William Potts

From a New England Hillside

William Potts

From a New England Hillside

ISBN/EAN: 9783744664769

Printed in Europe, USA, Canada, Australia, Japan

Cover: Foto ©Thomas Meinert / pixelio.de

More available books at **www.hansebooks.com**

FROM A NEW ENGLAND HILLSIDE

FROM A NEW ENGLAND HILLSIDE

NOTES FROM UNDERLEDGE

BY

WILLIAM POTTS

New York

MACMILLAN AND CO.

AND LONDON

1895

Norwood Press
J. S. Cushing & Co. — Berwick & Smith
Norwood Mass. U.S.A.

Can rules or tutors educate
The semi-god whom we await?
He must be musical,
Tremulous, impressional,
Alive to gentle influence
Of landscape and of sky,
And tender to the spirit-touch
Of man's or maiden's eye:
But, to his native centre fast,
Shall into Future fuse the Past,
And the world's flowing fates in his
    own mould recast.

— EMERSON.

FROM A NEW ENGLAND HILLSIDE.

———◆———

I.

I have not spent October in the country for nearly forty years : —

As one who long in populous city pent,
Where houses thick and sewers annoy the
   air, —

I roam among these hills and look out over the valleys with quite indescribable emotions.

Tears, idle tears, I know not what they
   mean,
Tears from the depth of some divine despair
Rise in the heart and gather to the eyes,
In looking on the happy autumn fields,
And thinking of the days that are no more.

How fortunate it is that some have been gifted with the power of expression, "that the thoughts of many hearts might be revealed." My friend objects to Sir John

Lubbock's "Pleasures of Life" for the same reason, though not from the same cause, that the old lady objected to Shakespeare — that it is made up of quotations. Now I wholly disagree with him. This is a work-a-day world, and blessed be the man with the time and happy taste to gather and put before us the choice bits which reveal us to ourselves.

The late rains of summer after a long drought made the fields and woods so green that the autumn glory has been long in coming, but is now spreading abroad so rapidly that one can scarcely keep pace with it. The fields are still full of flowers. On Sunday afternoon I noticed the following in one old pasture: Golden-rods and asters of various species, blind gentian, grass of Parnassus, thistles, spearmint, a lobelia, yarrow, wild carrot, brunella, fragrant ladies'-tresses (which White of Selborne calls ladies'-traces), life everlasting, purple polygala, thoroughwort, turtle-head, two kinds of knot-weed, wild strawberry, and a yellow flower which I ought to know but do not. On my way over that morning, I found a spot glorious with the fringed gentians, and during to-day's stroll I found them by the hundreds — yes, I think, thousands. I will not tell you where, for I want to keep that spot to myself.

I have also found the yellow oxalis, butter-and-eggs, dandelions, oxeyed daisies, cardinal flowers, water-cresses, looking for all the world like sweet alyssum, evening primroses, and others, and yesterday I was surprised to find the witch hazel in full bloom, the yellow leaves still mostly clinging to the stems, and last year's seed-vessels only turning brown. This is one of our most plentiful shrubs, and I am fond of its quaint irregularity. The hop hornbeam is another of our favourites among the shrubs or small trees, and these are found in company. A less satisfactory neighbour is the venomous swamp sumach, lovely but treacherous. Like the fringed gentians, — and fishing, — it is not to be found just here, but is all around us, and those who, like myself, are susceptible to its malignant power, must exercise caution in their interviews with it.

The golden-rods are past their prime, but this cannot be said of the asters, unless their mellow autumn is richer than their summer. The roadsides in some places are purple and in others white with them.

The chicken grapes hanging upon hedges

recall the spring fragrance of the blossoming vines, which vie with the ground-nut (Apios) of later summer in making scented aisles of our pathways. The berries of the bitter-sweet hang in golden clusters, but have not yet opened their hearts to the breeze, and the red hips of the wild roses promise to be with us all winter. Under the trees the berries of the mitchella are scattered thickly on the carpet formed by the round green leaves on the vines.

Our sounds are the sounds of the late harvest, and this is nearly over. The ripe corn is stacked in the fields, revealing golden pumpkins galore, with certainty of unending pies, while here and there a blossom shows that the vigour has not yet all gone out of the vines. The birds are mostly quiet, a catbird, with its noisy note, doing most to attract my attention during my morning walk. We shall see and hear more of the birds, but the cheery songs will only come to us again with the opening spring.

From my window I can hear the katydid's iteration all day long, — that terrible insistence, with the counter denial, which make you feel so sure that, whatever it was that was done or was not done in the long, long past, we never shall know the truth of the story while the world endures.

The morning was bright and sunny, and the hills and fields were all aglow. The humming wires along my way sent my memory back over more than forty years to the time when the telegraph, then a comparatively new contrivance, was built along the high road through my father's little farm in Pennsylvania. We youngsters listened to the messages going through, as we thought, and wondered that the birds could rest upon the wires with impunity. Perhaps this morning the wires were bringing to this peaceful spot some message of the desolation which has just been wrought in the distant South. But it is not always so peaceful even here. A month ago a great gale passed through and shattered some of our noble trees, and to-day the barometer has been falling, the afternoon has been overcast, and we expect to take our share in the common lot.

OCTOBER 6, 1893.

II.

THE night brought us only light and refreshing showers, though these were accompanied by the ripening leaves, which fell thick and fast, and strewed the ground this morning with a carpet of red and gold. But the sun came out between the clouds with his face washed clean for the holiday, and brought back with him the warmth of summer. As I passed down the village street I had to dodge the horse-chestnuts, which have become ripe enough to fall, and, bursting their burrs as they reach the path, scatter shell and nut on either side.

(And apropos, as I was writing this I became conscious of a bombardment in my room at intervals, the cause of which I found in something of the same nature. Yesterday I placed a flowering branch of witch hazel above my piano. The dry air of the room has rapidly matured the last year's fruit, and the shells opening from time to time with a snap, send the seed scurrying across the room to find an uncongenial resting place upon the table or floor.)

This has been a stirring and eventful week with us. Thursday was the opening day at the school, and the girls have been flocking back by ones and twos and threes and dozens, with trunks and bags and bundles, and the old-time lumbering stage and baggage wagons have been kept employed to the extent of their capacity. And not only the new girls, and those not new are here, but the ancients, the old timers, the girls of the past, who come only on account of old attractions and to meet each other and to see the new girls, are here in force, and have taken possession of the pleasant inn, and make its low-studded rooms resound with their busy chatter.

Beauty may indeed be only skin deep, but it warms the cockles of an old man's heart to see the lovely faces, and witness the fulness of life and boundless enthusiasm of these young maids. It may be confessed that it has a chastening effect upon him of the more muscular sex to see how absolutely independent of any of his kind are all of this body of Amazons. As he takes his accustomed course along the street he shrinks within himself, and manifests, quite involuntarily, a half apologetic air for showing himself unasked in such a goodly company.

I must add to my list of flowers still in bloom the slender gerardia, which I found this afternoon. My stroll took me up over the ledge and through the rocky sumach-covered pasture, where I kicked over now a yellow boletus, and now an Agaricus campestris, much the worse for wear, and wondered when our people would realize that they must know mushrooms as they know turnips before they eat them, and that then they could add very freely to the delicacies upon their tables.

My way led past our own reservoir, where the varied coloured trees, climbing the hill on the farther side, in the full glow of the westering sun, were reflected in the water, which, all of a tremor with a passing breeze, mingled their shades in a shimmer as of crinkled Venetian glass. — How odd it is, by the way, that we continually go to the artificial to find a simile for the natural effect which often so far surpasses it !

Leaving the crest of Rattlesnake Mountain on my left (how necessary it is for these hill towns to have a Rattlesnake Hill or Mountain in the neighbourhood — I hope

only as a survival in culture, an evidence
of a past industry), and wandering along
the soft, sandy road, I came to a tree where
the boys — presumably they were boys —
had been clubbing chestnuts, the prickly
burrs of which are now just opening. Of
course I picked up a stick and tried my
hand in the old way — just for a flyer, as it
were. And what a flyer it was indeed! It
reminded me of the way my sisters used to
do it, only I fear that the infrequency with
which the stick hit the tree would have excited the derision of even those well-mean-
ing maidens. The baseball player who
would have been able to "get on to my
curves," would have shown a miracle of in-
genuity. The net result of my industry
was two chestnuts, not by any means ripe,
I am sorry to say, but chestnuts nevertheless in the making. "While I was musing,
the fire burned." While I was chestnutting,
the sun sank behind the western hills, and
I hastened on, hoping soon to find my road
bending to the right and emerging into the
valley. But alas! what had been a well-
beaten country road with a stone wall on
one side, and a fence on the other, gradually
changed into a mere open cart track and
strayed away into the woods; first the

stone wall left me, and then the fence; instead of turning toward the valley I was gradually tending around the shoulder of the hill, and burying myself deeper and deeper in the woods. "And all the air a solemn stillness held," a silence which seemed no less a silence though it was full of the hum of crickets and other insects. By the way, have you ever lain awake at night, even in the depth of the winter, and found your ears filled with a humming and a rustling, until you wondered whether it would be possible to distinguish any other sound through it all, and then speculated whether there was really any sound — whether it was all the music of the spheres, whether it was external to you, whether it was the rushing of your own life's tide through your blood-vessels, or whether it was after all pure imagination?

The damp air of the evening, like the warm sun of midday, brings out the pleasant smell of the fallen leaves, and their rustle under the feet is agreeable; but I feared lest I was being caught in a cul-de-sac, or perhaps should be led out into the highway at too many miles' distance from home for so late an hour. I therefore retraced my steps, and was astonished to find the brightness of the lemon glow in the west, when I emerged from the shadowy aisles of the wood, while on the other side of me the flame-coloured leaves of the sassafras and the light yellow garments of the hickories and birches, relieved against their darker brethren, seemed the fore-runners of another day.

Passing along the road, here and there a warm breath from across the drier grass clove the cool, damp air of the gathering twilight; the glow on the sky changed from lemon to deep orange, against which the hills rested in nearly black masses; the glow narrowed, and above it in surprising brilliancy shone the evening star like a glittering gem, while in front rose our lovely tapering church spire, of which we are proud, — that familiar finger post of the Christian world which we all love whatever be the peculiarities of our various theories.

OCTOBER 7, 1893.

III.

This has been a typical autumn day; glittering and cool in the morning with high wind; thermometer fifty-six degrees; a clear blue sky gradually flecked with passing clouds; then heavier and denser masses, becoming more and more numerous until the whole heavens formed a leaden vault in delicately shaded tones, with here and there a break from time to time, through which the bright sun lighted up for a moment the tinted landscape.

I started to explore the woodland road wherein darkness overtook me last week. Passing through the village street, the fragrance of the late apples carried me back at once to the great show at Chicago. You cannot help remembering, if you were not so unfortunate as to have missed it, that the most refreshing experience at the Fair was a walk through the fruit-lined passages of the Horticultural Building, the delicious odour of the ripe fruit appealing more directly to your sense of *bien-être* than their magnificent size or gorgeous colour. It is well known, by the way, that the sense of smell awakens the memory and recalls the past through association of ideas more promptly than any other.

The road I was travelling passed, you will remember, to the westward of Rattle-snake Mountain. As it buried itself deeper in the wood, it likewise climbed higher, curving round and clinging to the side of the hill, here gently sloping. The fallen leaves, which were soft and moist last week, have now become crisp and much more numerous. Who does not delight in scuffling through them, and in the rustling sound, although this is anything but musical in the ordinary sense!

The foliage upon the trees has been thinned so much that the hillside shows massive rocks hitherto clothed with verdure, and from the summit protrudes in bold relief the rugged core of the mountain. Curving more and more to the left, the path emerged at length into an open field on the yonder side, in the midst of a herd of cattle peaceably grazing there; all around forest-clad hills, a very flower-garden in colour, with a depression on the northeast, where, in the middle distance,

the gilded dome of the Capitol shone in a
passing gleam of sunlight, against the blue
hills on the further side of the great river.
Skirting the edge of the wood, which for
a time shut off the view of the higher
ground, the path at length wholly deserted
me as I found myself near the foot of the
talus from the cliffs which formed the
summit.

I was left to take my chances among
the woodchuck holes, the hypothetical rat-
tlesnakes, and upon the sliding fragments
of rock. But remembering that the latter
naturally found for themselves a position
of stable equilibrium, I ventured upon
them with the care which every one is
bound to take in such a place, increased
to the nth power by the reflection of the
cautious man upon the serious predicament
in which he would find himself in case of
a mishap occurring in an unfrequented
locality.

Clambering around among great detached
masses of rock which stood out boldly midst
the trees, and speculating upon the possibility of in some way scaling the highest
of these, I became conscious of the pleasant odour of burning leaves, but also
apprehensive lest disastrous fire might be

running loose in the woods.　Approaching
a fissure among the rocks, however, I perceived a thin smoke issuing therefrom and
learned the source of the odour, and after
a few minutes I came in sight of two little
girls, to whom a pleasant "Good-morning"
introduced me sufficiently to obtain for me
an invitation to go into the "cave," where
Grandpa had just built a fire for their
delectation.

Grandpa proved to be a native, succes-
sor to several generations of such, sturdily
loyal to the neighbourhood and intelligently
familiar with its localities, characteristics,
and traditions.　The cave, which with a
little labour might be made into a comfortable enough residence, was formed of heavy
masses of basaltic rock leaning against each
other, and some hundred years ago it was
the occasional home of one of those "her-
mits" whom tradition has scattered through
the land, — restless geniuses, who, for one
reason or another, found it more to their
taste to "go back to nature" than to live
in houses made with hands.　This one bore
the distinction of having left a name behind him, and had been personally known
to the grandmother of my new friend.

My new acquaintance was quite an acquisition. By him I was led by a circuitous but easy path to the very highest point of the cliff, which had hitherto been quite concealed from me by the wood. Seen from this spot the horizon comes full circle, save as slightly broken here and there by the very tops of the most enterprising trees. It was formerly selected as a post for the observations of the coast and geodetic survey, and from it the eye takes in a thousand square miles of valley and rolling hills. As we stood on the bare summit, it blew a gale which it was difficult to withstand. The sun was shrouded with heavy clouds, and the miles on miles of forest-clad hills, and shaded valleys, among which the scattered fields seemed unimportant, showed the rich but soft and subdued colours of a well-chosen oriental rug. (Again that comparison of great things with small.)

We stood for a little while bracing ourselves against the wind, and noting the city a few miles away, and the scattered towns, becoming distinct now that the leaves are falling, with hills and mountains in every direction, none very high,—not more than fourteen or fifteen hundred feet, even in the extreme distance ; but the gale freshened, and making a mental note to come and come again to this point of vantage, I beat a retreat into the more sheltered valley.

I must add to the flowers still to be found, the red clover, the wild pepper-grass, and herb Robert. I never realized how beautiful the latter was until I found it to-day with its delicately divided leaves and lovely pink blossoms, emerging from between and overlaying the basaltic blocks over which I climbed. I cannot say so much in favour of its fragrance, but this was quite atoned for by the catnip against which I brushed on the hillside, and the sweet fern through which I waded near the summit.

OCTOBER 15, 1893.

C

IV.

Over the river, on the hill,
Lieth a village, white and still;
All around it the forest trees
Whisper and shiver in the breeze;
Over it sailing shadows go
Of soaring hawk and screaming crow,
And mountain grasses low and sweet
Grow in the middle of every street.

Over the river, under the hill,
Another village lieth still.
There I see in the cloudy night
Twinkling stars of household light,
Fires that gleam from the smithy's door,
Mists that curl on the river's shore;
And in the roads no grasses grow,
For the wheels that hasten to and fro.

THUS sang Rose Terry in her cottage
overlooking the river, and with that vision
always before her, I do not wonder that the
song came to her. On the steep hillside the
streets of white marble climb toward heaven
from the busy manufacturing village, and
their quietness in the broad glare of day

contrasts as strongly with the bustle below, if not so impressively, as under the cold light of the moon. My companion reminded me of the poem as our horses climbed the steep road, and told how the singer herself now reposes (as to the physical part) in that village on the hill where there's

Never a clock to toll the hours.

These people are as hospitable as one could ask to find. Here comes a good lady day after day and picks me up and carries me in the smoothest rolling of carriages far away among the hills, from which we can look back at our village at long range, or down into new valleys or over distant ridges. This time it was past Mrs. Rose Terry Cooke's former home, and by a winding river which tumbled and brawled over the rocks in pleasant fashion, and then upon a broad summit whence we could look over toward a region which, perhaps, from its contorted mass of hills and ridges, or perhaps from the unconventional habits or manners of its denizens has earned from the inhabitants of the neighbourhood the not too complimentary name of "Satan's kingdom."

Here and there still glows a brilliant

oak or maple, and now and then we see the whole gamut of colour on a sunlighted hillside, where the green leaves of the silver pines form a soft background for the brighter foliage. But many trees are bare, and show the full grace of their lines, and in numerous places we see as through a thin veil the secrets which the summer had concealed from our eyes.

I have repeatedly found myself after nightfall plodding along some unwonted wood path in the gathering darkness until I have begun to be apprehensive lest I might be compelled to pass the night in the damp, cool autumn air without shelter. On the last occasion I more than once nearly gave up extricating myself before morning. For these roads often start bravely with well-beaten tracks, but gradually show less and less evidence of use, and branch and branch until you are quite sure you do not know where you are. And the clouds cover the moon, and the darkness grows apace, and the shadows deepen about you; and you hear no sound save the katydids and crickets.

We have miles of woodland, broken here and there by open fields, and none of it primeval forest. Unhappily the primeval forest in this region is a thing of the past. Once in a while we see a fine old tree, usually in the village streets; an elm or a plane tree, a pine, a maple or an oak. But most of the wood is "second growth," or more frequently a third or fourth growth, and yet much cutting is going on, and some of it is very, very evil. These steep, rocky hillsides can never be made productive, and the removal of the forest covering will merely destroy their beauty and lead to the washing away of the slowly accumulated soil, and the consequent demoralization of the springs. In some places there are indications that former clearings are again growing up into wood but more frequently the young timber is being removed while of little value in itself. Occasionally the soil uncovered in the swales may be readily worked and made productive, but usually it is closely strewn with big and little masses of trap-rock which will forever render profitable cultivation practically impossible. And all the time you are conscious that the ground already cleared is inadequately tilled, and that a wise economy would turn all this labour into another channel.

As I walked through aisle after aisle of the Agricultural Building in Jackson Park, and examined the products of the great western farms, and the means by which these products were obtained, I wished over and over again that the farmers of New England could be with me, and see for themselves why it is that they do not meet with success in the old style of general farming, and why the competition in which they are engaged is necessarily a losing one, and New England shows so many "abandoned farms." I am sure there is a future for them, and a prosperous one, but it must be under other conditions, with a consideration of their situation and the character of the market.

I thought a few weeks ago that I had gathered my last fringed gentians, but I found a few to-day in my special preserve, opened wide to receive the comforting rays of the sun after last night's rain. I have left many to scatter their seed for next year, and I hope that the lovers of this beautiful flower will learn to keep their demands within moderate limits, for like the mayflower it threatens to leave frequented neighbourhoods. It is, I believe, a biennial, and not like the mayflower an evergreen perennial, and is therefore not so great a sufferer as that because of the ruthless dragging up by the roots to which it is exposed; but I have found a pair of pocket scissors not inappropriate in gathering it, and would modestly suggest to others the use of such, both for the fringed gentian and the mayflower.

To my list of plants in blossom must be added the charlock, the common and the French mullein, all found during the past week. But the flowers are rapidly becoming fewer. The asters are scarce and even the wild carrot, which continues so long to adorn the fields and roadsides with its beautiful lace-like blossoms, seems likely ere long to fail us. As the leaves fall, the orange berries of the bitter-sweet, of which we have a profusion, make more and more of a show, especially now that they have opened and exhibit the deeper orange of the ripe seeds within, while the red berries of the black alder gleam in the lowlands with their wonted brilliancy.

OCTOBER 28, 1893.

V.

I HAVE been re-reading Ruskin's "Elements of Drawing." He may be as bad an instructor as the art critics say, — I think perhaps he is, — but we cannot possibly do without him. Who has eyes if he has not? What a love for the facts of Nature! What a sense of the poetry of form and colour and motion! And what a vigorous pen and what strong muscular English! Yes, and what magnificent prejudices and splendid egotism! Reject all his instructions, if you like, and take some other course of study, but do not fail to read and ponder all that he has to say to you. And make sure that if you do not look at Nature as lovingly as he does, you will never do your best at finding out her secrets and revealing them (in confidence) to others.

By the way, I do not know anything else so preposterous as the claim made by some who assume a special love for the spectacle of Nature, of her glorious clouds and sparkling skies and sturdy trees and beau-

tiful flowers, — that you must bury yourself in ignorance concerning them, in order
to estimate them at their true value. With
great superiority they tell you that they
want to look upon the flowers and inhale their perfume, not to pull them to
pieces and find out how they are made ;
to watch the clouds rolling through the
heavens, not to know that they are masses
of sun-lighted vapour, and that the barometer is rising or falling. Is it so easy to un-
ravel the mystery of life ? Do you have
but to turn your hand, to discover that the
great earth as well as your small globe is
hollow, and that all dolls, big and little,
are stuffed with sawdust ? How petty the
awful universe must seem to such people !
Have they ever thought, after the ancient
poet, " When I consider the heavens, the
work of thy hands, the moon and the stars
which thou hast ordained, what is man that
thou art mindful of him, or the son of man
that thou regardest him ? "

I have sometimes watched those who
have expressed themselves as I have above
indicated, but I have failed to discover in
them any peculiar intensity of passion for
grace of form, glory of colour, smoothness
of melody, or richness of harmony. I have

failed to find that they bared their heads in more reverent awe before the majesty of the night, or thrilled with a greater tremulousness at loveliness of hue or delicacy of structure or fineness of tone, — at the rich life of the opening blossom, or the infinite expressiveness of the receding hills and valleys, fading away into the vast unknown of the distant horizon.

I do not mean that there are not some minds in which interest in a system or in a method of classification, takes the place of interest in the things classified. There undoubtedly are such dry-as-dusts in all departments of science — in all departments of life. A member of an important governmental commission has sometimes described a colleague as "always seeming more interested in the papers in a case than in the case itself." But this is nothing to the point. It takes all sorts of people to make up a world. You cannot know how much more enjoyment you could find in flowers and trees until you have looked into their history and studied their faces, learned their characters, their habits and their dispositions. You must lie down upon the same hillside, look up at the same sky, drink in the same air. You must learn to feel your oneness with them, and the strong family tie which makes everything that concerns them a matter of interest to you.

Novalis called Spinoza "a God-intoxicated man." Intoxication is not a pleasant word, — enthusiasm is better, — en-the-osiasm, — and it is this enthusiasm, the gift of Nature and the imagination combined, the offspring of poetry and fact, — that is the greatest, the richest, blessing of life. "I do not see in Nature the colours that you find there," said the lady to Turner. "Don't you wish you could, madam?" was the reply.

Suppose you try to look a little deeper, see a little further, turn the microscope upon your blossom, and discover a thousand beauties, the existence of which you had never suspected; turn your telescope upon the heavens, and find them bursting into bloom, — world beyond world receding into the vast, unfathomable depths of space; believe me, you will not become blasé with the extent of your knowledge, will not feel that the bloom is wholly gone from the peach, the perfume from the rose, the foam from the bounding wave.

It seems to me that I have frequently

heard talk about "the law of contradictories." I haven't the least idea what "the law of contradictories" means, but I think that, without serious trouble, I could define such a law. Ruskin says in this volume : "No touch or form is ever added to another by a good painter, without a mental determination and affirmation." The same day that I read this, I read in the introduction to "The Rosenthal Method of Practical Linguistry" : "No action can be done well which is not done unconsciously." Both are true statements; this is an illustration of the many-sidedness of life. If you have read the late William M. Hunt's "Conversations upon Art," you will remember that he asserts at one moment the diametric opposite of that which he strenuously insists upon at another. He is right : we must view both sides of the shield, if we would know it for what it is.

But how can I contend that that which is the result of a mental determination can be unconscious ? Easily. The time was, when the act could only be done consciously and painfully. But then, as Rosenthal says, it could not be well done. It must be " word upon word, line upon line, here a little and there a little," until both mind and hand are trained, not to do the thing in a perfunctory way, but to do it in the right way; to do one thing after another because such is the necessary order and relation, as the player upon a musical instrument often does perfectly, without looking, that which he would stumble over horribly if he should try to follow, note by note, as he did in the times which are past. That which he has learned has become embodied in his mental structure; it is now a part of his endowment, like the faculty of breathing or walking without thought of the process.

OCTOBER 30, 1893.

VI.

The frost this morning was not by any means the first of the season, but it was by much the most severe. The fields were almost as white as if a light snow had fallen, and each leaf and blade of grass was bordered with a delicate fringe of spicular crystals and encrusted with a coat of gems. The pools were frozen over, and here and there on the roadsides the ice took curious curly forms that seemed to defy explanation.

My morning stroll took me over the ledge and the hilltop, among the sumachs, cedars and young oak trees. My object was to ascertain whether the conical mountain upon our most distant horizon is actually that well-known peak which popular belief asserts it to be. But alas! it was the old story of the sun and the wind over again. Only here it was the delicate haze pervading the Indian summer air, which had effectually effaced the pile of rugged trap-rock of which I was in search, leaving for me alone — but how large an alone! — the glorious dissolving view of valley and distant hills under the warm November sun.

From the pastures I heard the cawing of the crows; upon a tree trunk near me hammered a woodpecker; afar through the wood resounded the regular stroke of an axe; and the pleasant odour of burning leaves tickled my nostril. But alas! we must sometimes pay dearly for our pleasures. Yesterday in driving along a picturesque wood road among wild and rocky hills, I crossed a line of fire, fully a third of a mile long, steadily marching through the fallen leaves, and eating up in its path shrubs and herbs, and the surface of the soil itself, with the upper roots and the innumerable seeds which had been shed upon it and buried within it. Merely from the wad from a sportsman's gun probably, but it was wiping out acre after acre of sylvan beauty, damaging to some extent the trees themselves, and leaving an ashy waste beneath them — and all to make an American holiday.

Then along comes the brave woodchopper, and down go the saplings and seedlings, chestnut and oak, maple and beach, pine and hickory, — and for what? Firewood, simply. Cord wood takes the place of the promising timber, which a little judgment would have left to attain respectable size, when by judicious selection and care it might be made to furnish a profitable annual crop, while the woodland should remain a beauty and a joy forever.

The wild flowers are now very scarce. This morning I found none but the witch hazel, the golden-rod, an aster, the wild carrot, chamomile, and pepper grass. A more extended and careful search would probably have been rewarded by buttercups and daisies (or white-weeds), — among the first to come and last to go, — by yarrow, chickweed and the mulleins, all of which I have found within two or three days. Even the fringed gentian showed a few of its lovely blue blossoms in a protected meadow only the day before yesterday, their third "last appearance" for the season. Dandelions I have heard of, but have not seen for several weeks. Doubtless we shall have them from time to time throughout the year. I have found them in the Brooklyn park in January and February.

We have now one of the greatest pleasures of which the leafy summer deprives us, the sight of the graceful stems and branches of the trees, with all their wonderful variety of angle and curve, of rugged strength and graceful flexibility ; the deeply scored trunks of the strong and massive oaks. the smooth bark of the beeches, with their pendulous branches, the sharp spines of the honey locust — a veritable " monkey puzzle " or natural cat-teazer, and the cork-winged twigs of the liquidamber.

And over the hillsides is that delicate warm glow of the young branches of this year's growth, which will become richer as the spring draws on, and life comes nearer and nearer to the surface, until a tender juicy green spray overspreads them all, gradually shrouding their delicate limbs from honest as well as vulgar eyes. This beauty of the trees comes to me as a revelation each day, " new every morning and fresh every evening," and I am sure that we ought to be of finer stuff than others, who have the privilege of seeing it, and seeing it against the limpid sky, not cut into squares and triangles and trapezes and dodecagons and whatnots formed by street lines and house roofs, but the very vault of heaven, resting with the softest, gentlest touch upon the distant hills, and throwing over us its wide protecting arch.

NOVEMBER 11, 1893.

D

VII.

WHEN I reached the station last evening on my return after a week's absence, I found the ground covered with snow, and the stage awaiting me on runners. The heavens were shrouded in cloud, a few flakes were falling, and the wind blew fiercely. But inside the closed conveyance we were snug enough — eight of us; and there was an unwonted pleasure in the gliding of the craft over the roads which had recently been rather rough and jolting.

This morning the scene was changed. Cowper's lines very nearly describe the situation : —

The night was winter in his roughest mood;
The morning, sharp and clear.

Indeed, a more perfect day for the season I do not believe ever blessed this goodly land. About five inches of snow covers the ground, in some places crusted over firmly enough to sustain one's weight by the freezing after Sunday's rain. " White as the driven

snow " is the received expression to describe
that which is perfectly spotless, and nothing is conceivable which in its kind could
be more perfect. Yet there is whiteness and
whiteness, as there are deacons and deacons.
As the angle varies at which you see it, so
varies the light reflected from it, and in this
gorgeous sunshine my shadow as it precedes
me over the fields is as deep and pure a blue
as the artists would make it.

What a friendly companion is this same
shadow ! The experiences of Peter Schle-
mihl appear perhaps a trifle extravagant,
and I am not willing to be responsible for
the statement that he actually did at one
time possess Fortunatus's purse, and con-
secutively *le nid invisible*, and the seven-
league boots ; but I am sure that he must
have had one or other or all these to console
him effectually for the loss of his friendly
shadow. How "closer than a brother" it
sticks to us, modestly walking behind when
we advance toward the sun, and throwing
itself boldly in our path as we turn our
back upon the light ! And how ridiculously
it imitates our slightest motion, a veritable
monkey as a mimic, and with the monkey's
delicacy of feature !

It is only upon the smooth lawns and

paths that the snow spreads a spotless,
unbroken sheet. On the open fields and
pastures it is broken by the stems of the
wild roses, bearing their brilliant red hips,
the hardhack, the wild carrot which fills
its cup with it, the fluffy seed-plumes of
the golden-rods. The branches of the trees
soon shake off its downy flakes, and, looking athwart the landscape, the pure white
spaces form but a minor part of the whole
scene, broken by house and fence and
woodland, which are clearly outlined against
its whiteness.

Clear as the air is, — the sun shining from
a cloudless sky, — the valley stretching away
at my feet in the afternoon becomes suffused
with mystic light as of Indian summer, and
as the day advances, the distant hills seem
to float in a warm haze in which they fade
away, carrying the eye to the limit of vision,
and leaving it fixed upon the glow which
shrouds but glorifies the far horizon.

Near by, the village spire is bathed in
the fading light ; no — I should not say fading light, for the sun is still above the
horizon, and the spire stands out clearly
against the sky. But it is the reverse of
Wordsworth's fading "into the light of
common day," — it is rather, as it were,

"trailing clouds of glory" that, lighted by the sinking sun, it lifts itself into the air above the tree-tops.

And the tree-tops themselves, those delicate sprays which now we see prodigally scattered around us, as if they were not "of beauty all compact," partake of the illumination, and to the very tips of their bud-crowned twigs thrill with the flooding light of the parting day.

DECEMBER 6, 1893.

VIII.

A NUMBER of my friends appear to be in a complete maze as to what inducement can be strong enough to lead me, in the dead of winter, to desert the pavements, the trolley cars, and the throng of the city for the hilly dirt-roads, the snow-covered wood-paths, and the rocky hillsides of the country. A great portion of our reading and thinking people, or those whom we deem such, seem to have become cockney to the core. In nothing perhaps is the modern tendency toward urban life more strikingly shown than in this change of mental attitude wrought by habit and association, this loss of appreciation of the delights of rural life. I sincerely trust that the wave has reached its highest point, and that ere long we shall begin to see a reaction toward a more healthy ideal.

After the warm sun and rapid thaw of yesterday, I woke this morning to find the air full of the soft falling snow, and the discoloured track in the middle of the road

again decently covered with a veil of white.
The snow continued to fall throughout the
morning, not heavily, but steadily, and
toward noon, covering myself with a long
mackintosh, I sallied forth to get the benefit
of it at first hand. I took the mountain
road : on the left the ground fell away rather
gently to the broad intervale, while on the
right, beyond a narrow valley, at a few
hundred yards' distance, the hillside rose
steeply to the height of several hundred feet,
— here covered with dense wood, and there
by scattered trees and rocks, now and then
accented by a bold cliff; the ground all
robed in white, and the trees, especially the
numerous evergreens, singly or in groups,
all heavily weighted with their downy garments.

"Fast fell the fleecy shower." There
were as yet only two or three inches of new
fallen snow, and walking, though warm
work, was not very difficult, as it would
have been had the snow been deeper. Travelling on foot in heavy snow, though excit-
ing and exhilarating, is hard enough for a
man ; for a woman, with skirts, it must be
something appalling. One of my neighbours
told me last night how in her girlhood she
had suddenly been seized one day with a

desire to see how the wood looked in winter. She started alone, and had travelled some distance from the house before she realized what she had undertaken. The weather was mild, and the snow was up to her knees; but she struggled on, becoming hotter and hotter, but fearing to stop for a moment to rest. The work became heavier and heavier as her strength diminished; she was a mile from shelter, and discomfort gradually gave place to alarm and something approaching terror. There was nothing to be done but to struggle on through that unending lonely waste, which yet ended at last, when, completely exhausted, she found herself again under a friendly roof. And how did the wood look in winter? Alas! she had to confess to her sisters that she not seen the wood through which she had made her way; the burden of the walk had been much too great.

We see what our minds are fixed upon, and we consciously see little else. Occasionally, I think, visions come back to us of scenes which we have not noticed at the time, which have yet in some way recorded themselves upon the tablets of the mind. But ordinarily we see and hear that with which our thought is concerned. Have you not ever been in a great factory, where the whirr of the machinery and the din of the hammers filled the air as though all bedlam had broken loose, until it seemed, as the common saying is, that you could not hear yourself think, and yet, after a little time, found that you could, when you would, discriminate a particular sound, now one, and now another, — apparently a solo with an accompaniment? Or in a well-balanced chorus, have you not sought a certain voice and followed it through the labyrinthine harmony? So with sight, but to a much greater degree, and with much more important and very potent results.

Tramping over the hills south of the village a few weeks ago, on a very sunny morning, my attention was drawn to a sloping pasture, over which, as is the case with numerous others in the neighbourhood, there were scattered many tiny cedars. As I have said, the morning was sunny, and these dense cedar bushes cast dark shadows on the hillside. These shadows first caught my eye, and I was suddenly conscious of a field covered with dark spots, without any immediate conception of the cause. My reason being excited to activity, I at once realized the objects casting the shadows, and as I did so, the shadows themselves lost their prominence and almost passed from notice. And so for a few moments I stood, amusing myself with seeing first shadow, then object, then shadow, as my mind turned from one to the other, and it was only with a certain effort of the will that I could attain what might be called a comprehensive view of the scene, bringing its various elements into due relation.

In this, it seems to me, there is a not unimportant lesson touching the art of the day. Art in painting is Nature seen through trained human eyes, and interpreted by skilled human hands. The human and individual element in it is the essential element, and true art must be as varied as are the individuals through whom it comes to us. Just what I see, my friend does not see; and just the impression that it produces upon me is not the impression that it produces upon him. But we are the servants or interpreters, and not the masters of Nature, and we must try to see truly, in our own way, and not falsely. Is this what all our artists do? Is it not rather with many of them, that they seek for the bizarre, — for a *reductio ad absur-*

dum? Receiving a certain impression from Nature which they have not noticed before, do they not straightway fal' down and worship it, and, forsaking all others, cleave only unto that, to the destruction of their art and their own usefulness?

Monet looks at a haycock in the broad sunlight of a summer's day, and sees that on the edges of the grass blades the rays of light are broken into the prismatic colours! Presto! the harvest field goes off in a blaze of theatrical glory. The ninety-nine per cent of the neutral tints are swept into the limbo of nothingness, giving place to a dust heap of broken rainbows, on a crumpled field of crude pigments; and all the mysterious soft intricacy of Nature, with its delicacy of suggestion, its harmony and repose, are gone forever.

I do not mean that these men (I only use Monet's name as an instance) have nothing to tell us, but merely that what they have to say they tell in such a way as to convey a false message; they sacrifice themselves, their art, and the interests entrusted to them, by a false perspective. They fail to see truly through their own eyes, or else fail to report truly what they see, which latter is the proper function of

the artist, qualified only by the proviso,
that he must always see something fine,
beautiful, ennobling, or helpful.

But I was climbing the hillside through
the fast-falling flakes. Crossing the crest
of the ridge between the files of hooded
cedars, standing —

Muffled and dumb like barefoot dervishes,

the road wanders down across a lateral
valley through which runs the "Great
Brook," — then climbs the hill beyond,
sinks into another valley, and toils up
through the closer wood towards the top
of the ridge. At the crossroads I stop and
hearken. There is no wind, and not a sound
breaks the silence excepting the soft alight-
ing of the snow, and the dull rumble of a
train of cars upon a railroad five or six
miles away. As I listen, the latter fades
in the distance beyond the hills to a scarcely
perceptible murmur, and nothing is left but
the sound of the falling flakes, now gradually changing to sleet, and beginning to
make a Liliputian rattling upon the crisp
leaves of the oaks and beeches. Between
the trunks and branches of the trees my
eye wanders down into the valley ; the
woodlands, the fields, and the lines of wall

and fence become more and more blurred and vague, and before reaching the hills which mount beyond, sink into the bosom of the thick atmosphere which shuts us in from the noise and bustle of the outer world.

FEBRUARY 9, 1894.

IX.

I AM a thorough believer in temperance. Perhaps temperance is a more or less elastic term. It is universally understood that this climate of ours is a temperate climate. Yesterday morning the thermometer stood at five degrees below zero; this morning it stood at forty-five degrees above. It is in averaging these that you find the temperance. Temperance seems to require an accent, and the accent yesterday morning was quite sharp.

"Give me neither poverty nor riches," was the prayer of Agur. And we all say Amen, — but sometimes we find the accent too low, and sometimes too high — though, to tell the truth, we rarely notice the latter. Each of us, at least, is sure that Agur was quite sound when he continued, "Feed me with food convenient for me." About this there is no mistake, and we know what is convenient.

And, after all, I am convinced that when we have gone the round of a goodly assortment of viands, there are certain stand-bys which are pretty sure to be acceptable day in and day out; and roast beef is very good as a steady diet, if only now and then we can have just a soupçon of horseradish to make the accent. *In medio tutissimus ibis*, but we hardly know how much we are enjoying ourselves there unless now and then we have an opportunity to knock our shins against the curbstone on one side or other of the path.

Homekeeping youth have ever homely wits,

and in the endeavour to avoid this reproach in my own case, I once upon a time made a voyage to the Bermudas. And such a voyage! Was it ever your fortune to cross the Gulf Stream in January or in February on board the Trinidad or the Orinoco? If it was, nothing more needs to be said. Since that time, when I have made the stormy passage in the frail ferry-boats between New York and Brooklyn, or risked the waves of the wild Atlantic on the way to Staten Island, I have thought of the revolutionary efforts of that other craft in the Sargasso Sea, and have contented myself with the spice of memory as a sufficient flavour for the mild joys of the present.

And, if need be, I am sure that it will last me for my time. Have I not been in foreign parts? Have I not lived under strange skies and looked upon strange waters? And what waters! Ah! when I remember that first hour in Castle Harbour, after the terrible voyage, it seems to me that I then attained the impossible. If that actually was, there was nothing which might not be. The common, every-day world was no more, for I was in Shakespeare's "still vex'd Bermoothes."

By the way, is it not odd that we are in the habit of placing the scene of " The Tempest " in the Bermudas, when that is almost the one sole spot of all the globe which Shakespeare excludes? Ariel says : —

> Safely in harbour
> Is the king's ship; in the deep nook, where once
> Thou call'dst me up at midnight to fetch dew
> From the still-vex'd Bermoothes, there she's hid:
> The mariners all under hatches stow'd:
> Whom, with a charm join'd to their suffer'd labour,
> I have left asleep; and for the rest o' the fleet,
> Which I dispers'd, they all have met again,
> And are upon the Mediterranean flote,
> Bound sadly home for Naples.

But it doesn't make any difference; we know that we are on the island of the wise Prospero and the gentle Miranda; we hear Ariel, that tricksy spirit, in the tamarisk trees among the ragged rocks by the beach, singing : —

Come unto these yellow sands,
And then take hands:
Court'sied when you have, and kiss'd
(The wild waves whist,)
Foot it featly here and there;
And, sweet sprites, the burden bear.

Or else —

Full fathom five thy father lies;
 Of his bones are coral made;
Those are pearls that were his eyes;
 Nothing of him that doth fade,
But doth suffer a sea change
Into something rich and strange.
Sea-nymphs hourly ring his knell;
Hark! now I hear them, — ding-dong bell!

And we are just as sure that Caliban made his home in the Devil's Hole as we are that his dam's god Setebos once ruled the island. It is simply impossible to realize that you are on a part of the common work-a-day world. The shell roses and freesias bloom at your feet; the rich bou-

E

gainvillea drapes your doorway; royal
palms wave over your path; the loveliest
maiden-hair ferns hangs a curtain at the
roadside; under the pearly waves the corals
blossom, and around you stretches a waste
of waters — a million square miles without solid land so much that a fly could rest
his foot upon it. And as you listen to the
wind blowing against your upper window at
the Hamilton, you momentarily expect the
whole mysterious structure to sink beneath
you : —

And, like this insubstantial pageant faded,
Leave not a rack behind.

But this, you will think, is not that temperance of which I spoke. Ah! but it is
the spice, the nectar, the little touch of
pure colour among the neutral tints which
brings the whole together and makes every
most insignificant part as essential as every
other. Do I want Burgundy every day?
Must I go from birds of paradise to night-
ingales' tongues; seek for turbot in the
pools in the intervale, and gather manna
from the top of Rattlesnake Mountain?
Nay. Tartarin may go hunt his lions in the
desert or creep upward upon the arête of
the Weisshorn or the Matterhorn, but I — I

have seen the world. Henceforth I may rest at Underledge, looking out upon the valley. I know that the river runs fast between its banks, though the elms and maples quietly stand guard by its side and conceal it from my view; the snow lies white over the fields, and beyond, the hills climb skyward to meet the brave cloud fleets sailing the ocean blue. Softly the retreating lines sink into each other in the gray distance; no musical note reaches my ear. I only catch the distant bark of a dog or the crowing of a cock; but I close my eyes, and lo! the angel fish sparkle in the pools at Westover; the roses bloom again by my side, and the air is rich with their perfume; the waters, emerald and gold and turquoise, lap the sands at my feet, and I hear Ariel singing : —

Where the bee sucks, there suck I;
In a cowslip's bell I lie;
There I couch when owls do cry.
On the bat's back I do fly
After summer, merrily:
Merrily, merrily, shall I live now,
Under the blossom that hangs on the bough.

FEBRUARY 18, 1894.

X.

By the force of circumstances I was obliged to spend in the great city the day dedicated to the memory of the Father of his country, and having much writing to do, I spent the greater part of the day at the club.

And what, of its kind, could be pleasanter? I may take mine ease in mine inn, but where, excepting by his own fireside, can one so thoroughly take his ease, and feel so completely how good life is, as he can in the library of his club, — provided his club is our club? Around him are ranged tier above tier the goodly volumes to which he may refer if necessity require; upon the desk before him are all the conveniences for his labour; the temperature is just right; the light falls over him broadly and softly; the admonition to "silence" faces all as they enter the room; the heavy carpet and rugs deaden the footfalls; and as the student from time to time raises his eyes, they rest here and there upon the poet, the painter, the musician, the divine, the man of affairs, each at home and each an equal citizen of this true republic, following the bent of his own inclination quietly and undisturbed.

When my stint had been accomplished, and the time for relaxation had arrived, soothed by the sense of leaving a completed task, what reward could possibly be more inviting than a soft easy-chair beside an incandescent lamp, and the latest instalment of the serial story for which we all impatiently wait from month to month?

In these latter days we have heard much of naturalism, and especially of naturalism in fiction, and there seems to have been a very strong assumption upon the part of many that naturalism is necessarily nasty. I repudiate the thought with all the vigour of my being. Nature is pure, and nothing can compare for naturalism with purity. Give us the blue skies, the fresh winds, the sturdy trees, the dainty flowers, the bright clean souls and loving hearts.

"Tis as easy now for the heart to be true
As for grass to be green or skies to be blue,
"Tis the natural way of living.

Let us drink deep draughts of this naturalism, — we can ask nothing better. But do not forget to flood it with the glow of imagination ; that also is natural, and the highest thing in Nature, — and Zola himself, deep as he may burrow, dare not venture to despise it.

We often complain of the unsatisfactoriness of reading serial stories, but there is something to be said on the other side. It is somewhat in these as in the romances of our own lives, and the lives of those whom we see around us ; we are present and observant while character and fate are making, and from month to month we await the unfolding of the drama, as we wait in suspense for the thing that shall be. The members of the cast have taken their places upon the stage ; the curtain is up, — the action proceeds. What is to be the fate of these new friends of ours ? Let us not anticipate ; let us wait and see.

In the evening I looked upon quite a different scene. The Neighbourhood Guild in the sister city had a little entertainment in honour of the day at its modest home down near where they build the big ships which carry the nation's flag over the broad seas. When the time for refreshments came, there were seated at the tables

perhaps a hundred, of all ages and both
sexes, gathered from homes where comfort
abounds, where friends and books and pictures and meat and drink can be had when
they are wanted, and from homes, some of
which can perhaps be identified as such
only by remembering the saying that
"home is where the heart is." And perhaps in some of these places — who knows ?
— even that redeeming feature may be
wanting. But here all were on common
ground, and good fellowship, contentment
and happiness shone on every face.

The presiding officer at the simple feast
was one still young, from a neighbouring
home, who a few years ago, when the enterprise took form, was among the first to
accept, rather distrustfully, the invitation
of those who had ventured to invade the
region. Now, thoroughly imbued with its
spirit, he is one of the strongest of the con-
necting links in this social chain.

"But," says my good friend Blondin at
the club, "you have convicted yourself with
your own pen. You have been lauding the
Arcadian life at Underledge and inviting
us to leave our comfortable clubs and our
municipal experiments and follow you out
among the hypothetical shepherds on your

dreary hills ; but now you have been compelled to flee to the city, and under the inevitable revulsion of your feelings you are
obliged to paint in glowing colours the very
advantages which we are constantly holding
up to your view. What have you to say to
this ? "

Just this, O Blondin, I reply. Though I
have sought the fields, the woods and the
hills, I have not therefore deserted your club,
and my club, have I ? Nor have I ceased
to be one of those who are at home at the
Guild, one whose co-operation is as welcome there as in the Current Topics Club
at Underledge. But this is not the whole.
There is a time for all things under the sun.
And there is social life, culture and enjoyment even at Underledge.

Yesterday the wind came out of the north,
and it waxed high, and the mercury fell, and
it fell, and it fell. But the stars were in the
sky, and we all gathered at the town hall, for
there the Troubadour was to recite stories to
us, and to sing to us the Creole songs. And
he told us about the charming Narcisse and
his wonderful skill in Chi-og-aphy, and phy-
siognomy, and how he ever abstained from
borrowing (*a gauche*), and how fond he was
of gay clothing ; but also how he went

bravely to his death at last, one of the innumerable offerings upon the altar of the lost cause.   And he told us how the coy Widow Riley was won at last.   And we heard the drum beat once more, and we that were old enough remembered anew those long and weary days and nights which seemed as though they would last forever, but which are now so far away in the past that the young folks around us can look upon them as they can upon the times of Cambyses and Alexander.

And then he ended with the story how Mary made her way through the lines in the darkness of the night, whereat Phillis and Phollis honestly bubbled over.   And then we four went out under the stars, and the heavens were all covered from the zenith to the horizon with mystic lambent flames, which pulsed and flashed and throbbed and glowed, while we stood and watched them with wonder and awe.   To Phollis it was, moreover, a revelation ; for the first time she gazed upon this splendour.

Then we passed on to the temple of learning, but, behold ! the door was shut both to the foolish virgins and the foolish men. And so we wandered along the slippery way, in the face of the icy blast, which was not so very cold after all, though the thermometer was at five degrees above zero (it was at six degrees below, this morning), until we reached the hospitable portal of Madame Liquidambar, which Mademoiselle quickly opened to us.

And there we found a fire of logs blazing upon the hearth, around which we all gathered, and the Troubadour discovered a guitar, which he strung, and upon which he played while he sang the song of Suzette, and then another and another and another, until it was quite time for us to start if we were to get home with the girls before the morning.

And Phollis asked why it was that the Scribe always seemed so happy, and the Scribe could not tell for the life of him, unless it was because he enjoyed so many things, and enjoyed them so much.

FEBRUARY 24, 1894.

XI.

EUREKA! Shall I say it? Nothing less would seem appropriate after the mile upon mile that I have rambled and scrambled and tangled this afternoon in search of the trailing arbutus. I have been in the most probable places, and I think that I may frankly say in the most uncomfortable. The climax was capped when I found myself upon a hillside in the midst of a wood of shrubs and saplings, over which fire had evidently passed within a few years, so weakening the young trees that they had subsequently fallen under the stress of storms, and lay crossed in all directions, with frequent briars among them, as always happens after a fire in the wood. Once caught in such a tangle, progress seems almost hopeless, and no inducement is offered to return. In that direction you know it is bad; there is always something to be hoped for in the unknown. And so I struggled onward, tripping and slipping, the twigs springing back and striking my glasses, the thorns clinging to me

closer than a brother. But even such uncomfortable places as these have a boundary, and that boundary I reached at last,
and I breathed freely and would have felt
wholly repaid had I but found what I
sought.

But courage! Just over there, upon that
southward facing wooded slope, is the spot
of spots for the vine that I seek. And
again a climb and a scramble, and while
clinging to the rocky and precipitous hillside I find a bit of saxifrage with its whorl
of green leaves, crowned with a little but-
ton of white flowers, just coming into bloom,
and nestling snugly close to the ground, not
proudly standing erect upon a six-inch stem,
as it would have been a little later, if I had
not plucked it out of the crevice in the rock
and carried it off home. And here is our
sole cactus, the prickly pear, not in bloom,
but almost looking as if it were, some of
the fleshy lobes having a bright pink tinge.
I pulled up two or three specimens to bring
with me, to the decided detriment of my
fingers, and had to spend most of the re-
mainder of the afternoon in pulling out the
prickles, which engaging occupation I transferred to Cara mea when I intrusted one of
the Tartars to her at the tea table.

But this was not the mayflower, and there below me wound the river, and yonder was the bridge which should bear me over the first limb of the horseshoe (if horseshoes have limbs. What is it that horseshoes have, — arms or limbs?). I took my way homeward, mourning, for I had not found it, and the day was overcast, and the sun was shrouded in gloomy clouds, and generally speaking my cake was dough.

Up in my own wood this morning I gathered a little cluster of hepaticas, — squirrel cups, I like to call them, — blue and white, and as dainty as you could possibly think. They made their appearance a fortnight ago, while the snow still lingered in shady places on the northern slopes, so early that Phollis said they could not venture out without their furs on, the dear little things. The columbines are showing their leaves, and the dogstooth violets and a few others, but excepting the symplocarpus (the euphemistic name of the skunk-cabbage) and the chickweed, I have seen no other wild herbs in blossom. Of trees and shrubs there are a number, the maples, the elms. etc., but most of the vegetable family are biding their time well. They were not beguiled by the lovely days of early March, and here, at least, the bitter winds of a week ago found few victims.

As I tramped across the fields this afternoon and looked at the evidences of the patient toil that had been spent in preparing them for the production of the scanty crops which can now be wrung from them, I wished that some of our closet philanthropists who are very wise upon the subject of taxes — in books and speeches — and who talk glibly on the relation of land and improvements and the unearned increment, would just once in a while take to the country and look at the thing itself. (I am sure that I am talking quite correctly, and in the true orthodox philosophical fashion, when I say "das ding an sich.") Here is land which, with the buildings upon it, might bring in the market perhaps fifteen dollars per acre. To say that labour to the extent of fifty dollars per acre had been expended upon it to fit it for the pasturage or other service that is now obtained from it, in clearing it of trees and shrubs, in removing and piling up the stones in long walls and heaps, or in digging great holes and trenches in which to bury them — which is, I find, a favourite way here of getting rid of them — would be to make a very modest statement.

And this is what the great leader of this school considers an immaterial item; the improvements upon land are the buildings. Well, what these buildings cost, I do not know. People live in some of them and house their cattle in others. I am quite sure that upon some farms the cattle have the better time. I have been in three or four of the houses. When I started out last summer I thought that I wanted an "abandoned farm." I did not take one.

But this is a side issue. Did you hear the frogs to-day? Not the great croakers with their hoarse voices calling out strange threats to frighten small children, but the musical little fellows, singing in all the swampy places that "Spring has come!" "Spring has come!" "Spring has come!" I heard them first less than two weeks ago, and their cheery note was as inspiring as that of the birds.

And the birds are here too, — the bluebird and the song sparrow, the robin and the red-winged blackbird, and a host of others, making merry early in the morning and late in the day, and I dare say going a-courting as young folks will. About the house, Chanticleer and Mrs. Chanticleer, or the Mesdames Chanticleer, have changed their note, and the lady vociferously tells the whole town what she has been about, "so early in the morning."

Ah, well — one generation passeth away and another cometh, and if the future is not for us, but for those that are to follow, is there anything sweeter in life than to try to make the world wholesome and lovely to live in, and to give the newcomers a fair start upon their journey onward and up-ward?

APRIL 1, 1894.

XII.

Our old village cherishes its comparative
seclusion, and it has been with somewhat.
jealous, though withal kindly feelings, that
it has listened for the past year to the more
or less audible murmurs of a proposed in-
vasion by the all-conquering "trolley."
Should we lose our rather distinctive character as a place apart, an old-fashioned New
England village of farmer-folk, where once
in the days of stage coaches and post-roads,
merchandizing was active, but which in the
new railroad era had been left as an aside,
dedicated to studious repose, and freedom
from the world's annoy? This was not an
unimportant question to many, both of such
as were to the manor born and had grown
up with the place, and such as had been
beguiled hither by the characteristics by
which it is marked. Our school, which has
been for many years under one successful
management, insomuch that it is famed
throughout the land, is our joy and our
pride, even if we do not all quite realize it,

F

and we view all changes as they may affect that centre of our activities.

But the day of debate seems to be over-past, and that of experiment is rapidly ap-proaching. The posts and ties lie along our northern street, and we hear that the unfruitful trunks, which are nevertheless hereafter to bear the lightning, have been planted close up to our borders. The neigh-bouring city is to be admitted to a glimpse into our Eden, and expectantly, though a little coyly, we await the approach of its citizens. Do not, we pray them, bring with you your city habits and city ways to mar the fair tablets of our rural simplicity. Come but as men and brothers (and sisters), and we will receive you with open arms. But remember that we are unsophisticated folk ; that we do not know the wiles of the great world, and that we rely upon you to cherish as your motto, *noblesse oblige*, and not abuse our ignorance and (comparative) innocence.

It has been one of my fancies that per-haps the extension of the electric railway lines throughout our rural districts, in which they seem to be forming, as it were, vast spider webs, might turn out to be one of our greatest blessings, in serving to scatter

the population which year after year has
tended more and more to gather into the
cities and great towns. If this may indeed
be so, and thereby the congestion may be
relieved, which has forced the municipal
problem upon us as one of the most serious
of the dangers which we have been compelled to face, we cannot be too grateful,
even though there be drawbacks which
somewhat temper our joy. The age of electricity, succeeding the age of steam, and
suddenly developing with an almost blind-
ing flash, finds us in an attitude of wonder,
anticipation, and awe. Is there any limit
to the direction and extent of the channels
which this delicate and powerful agency
will open? We are whirled from one development to another so rapidly that we
have no opportunity to assimilate them in
our consciousness, and a new application
of this multiform power is old and hack-
neyed before it has a chance to be even a
nine-days' wonder.

And what possibilities of disaster are we
laying up for ourselves with all this men-
agerie of partly tamed denizens of the wild
which we are trying to hold in leash?
Chained in great storage houses, sent flashing through the air or through the ground

or under the water in every direction, on what mad errand may they sometime go, if once the native instinct get the better of our imperfect control! Perhaps it may grow to be an everyday matter, and safe experience may remove all apprehensions; but the old-fashioned among us, while accepting gladly all the aid which this new servant is bringing us, cannot quite feel sure that he is not merely biding his time for a day of reckoning when all scores shall be paid off.

I have actually found it, — the mayflower, I mean. This morning I made another expedition, not so long as that of a few days ago, but more successful than that. It is true that the clusters of blossoms were small, and that there were more buds than blossoms, and more vines than buds, but nevertheless there were the delicate fragrant pink blossoms in fact, and one blossom contains the promise and potency of a world of delight. The most trying experience of the morning was the finding of a mile of woodland freshly burned over, in the very heart of what should have been my best foraging ground. I saw the fire across the valley two days ago, and I thought it was merely that the farmers were engaged in burning brush. But it was probably a railroad fire, one of the thousands upon thousands that occur every year all over the land, destroying millions of dollars' worth of valuable property, and impoverishing the soil over which they run. Is it not about time that the railroad corporations were compelled to take care that such disasters should not occur? It is not as if they could not be prevented. They can be, and that without serious difficulty. It is merely because we are only partly civilized that we permit them.

To-day the Easter holidays are ending, and the girls are trooping back to us, rejoicing, as I am sure they always do, at regaining their freedom among these hills, though perchance with hearts aching a little from the home partings. Then a few more busy weeks at the books while all sorts of distractions are calling upon them from without, the whole world waking up again to a new life, the white and fleecy clouds floating in the blue sky, tree and shrub and herb rushing exuberantly into blossom, the birds singing, and the bees humming; while the steady old earth, which has already seen so many, many summers, revolves upon its axis — shall I say, like a turkey on a spit?

—no, that would be quite too material; like nothing but its dear own self, bringing every part in time under the flood of sunshine pouring joy into the veins, as it were liquid fire, like unto the ichor of the gods.

APRIL 5, 1894.

XIII.

I was absent from home at the time of the great storm on the eleventh, and on my return yesterday found the snow only scattered in patches instead of completely covering the country as it had done two or three days before. Yet even this morning there were some drifts remaining of a foot or two in depth. With the temperature above sixty degrees, however, these cannot last long.

My morning walk was rewarded by a good handful of hepaticas, together with two or three yellow stars of the cinque-foil, which I found on a sunny slope, its first appearance. This afternoon I found many buds of the dog's-tooth violet just ready to open, though none quite expanded. At sunset the air was full of the ringing musical notes of the frogs. I suppose one should rather call it a chirping than singing, but by whatever name it be called, it is very pleasant to those that are fond of it. I heard them first as I neared the bed of the old canal, which the rapid thawing of the snow had refilled. They were all talking at once in the merriest humour possible; but though I approached quietly, and then stood still, they gradually became conscious of my presence, and, fearful lest I should betray their secrets, one by one fell into silence, until at length all had become as still as mice. Shortly after I had passed on, I heard them take up the tale again, narrating, I suppose, each after his own fashion, how "The frog he would a-wooing go."

The smaller river is out again over its banks, but the water has run off with surprising rapidity, and no damage will be done. The frost being all out of the ground, much water has soaked in, to our relief, and we shall begin the season with the springs well filled.

I brought with me from the city the architect's plans, specifications, etc., for the cottage that is to be, and the business now begins to take on a serious aspect. I have often amused myself as I have looked between the uncovered ribs of a skeleton house, with imagining the life that should be lived therein, its joys and sorrows and various incidents, and birth and death.

And now I look through the vacant space on the terrace upon the hillside, within the boundaries which I have roughly marked by four fragments of trap-rock, and all the multitudinous interests and queries of human life rise before my imagination.

Can we see the ghosts of what is to be, as well as of what has already been? So far no very terrible ghosts have appeared to me. It seems easy to think of the cottage as growing naturally out of the ground, the moss-covered masses from the ledge and the old stone fences taking their places in the walls, and offering a welcome to the vines that may come to cling to them. And the sunlight will stream easily through the broad windows, and glow upon book and picture, where now the free winds play and leave no track. And music of dulcimer and of sackbut and psaltery and harp in their modern concentrated form will take the place of the winds that whistle free, and mayhap the wind itself, moulded upon delicate vocal cords, may sing the finer airs of the great human composers.

And where now there are only flashes of light and pulses of free air, there may perchance be flashes of thought, gleams of imagination, heroic impulses. For who knows but some of the great ones may stray thitherward? And even if they do not, there may be at least brave hopefulness and honest endeavour and a helpful spirit. And if there should hap to be at times unsatisfied longings, and even a weary cry, that is but the common lot, and without these the life would hardly seem human.

But I am a poor prophet if in that dwelling which is yet unborn the sunny days shall not be more numerous than the sad days. Whence we come we know not; whither we go we know not. And it is said that "man is born unto trouble as the sparks fly upward." Yet in this little space between the silences, is there a great flood of life with which the whole universe pulses; over us is the blue vault of heaven with its spinning worlds, world beyond world, to the outer reaches of the imagination; the soil and the surface of the rock and the depth of the waters are budding and blossoming and seeding from hour to hour; the light waxes and wanes in infinite gradations of loveliness; the waters roar and the tempests wail, but anon delicious music fills the air and soothes the heart; it is given to us to feed our minds with all that is and was and shall be, and human heart touches heart, even though tongue be mute, and there may seem to be between one and another a great gulf fixed.

And so though we stand in the awful · presence of the unknown, and looking backward see nought but an impenetrable shade, and looking forward, behold only a golden haze; though there be days of pain and doubt and sorrow; though the grasshopper may sometimes seem a burden; yet shall the warm blood of the life that is fill the veins, and health and peace will come in the frank acceptance of the experiences that are sent, while the torrent is tamed, the winds are tempered, and the rough places are smoothed before those that are to come after.

APRIL 15, 1894.

XIV.

THE wild flowers have been slow in showing themselves, having doubtless learned
caution from past experience, but the week
just gone, with its many hours of warm
sunshine, followed by soft April showers,
has brought great changes. Within two or
three days I have found, besides the hepat-
ica, the first comer, the cinque-foil, the
dandelion, the common chickweed, shep-
herd's purse (is the size of the seed vessels
of this a true indication of the small wants
or only of the small attainments of the
pastoral part of the community ?) the dog's-
tooth violet in quantity, the bloodroot, the
lovely, modest little quaker lady or innocence, and the purple trillium, which has not
very often happened in my path in the
times that are gone. Nothing could be
more dainty than the houstonia — the little
quaker lady. And it is very trustful and
confiding withal, and will bloom just as
courageously and perseveringly in a saucer
at your window if you take up a clump of

it, and keep it properly moistened. It is a thirsty little creature, but then it only drinks the most harmless of beverages. One of my neighbours found a root of it as late as Thanksgiving Day last year, and put it into a tiny vase, which was lent to me for a few days more than a month ago, crowned with over fifty delicate blossoms, just touched with a tint of the vernal sky.

A marvellous change has taken place in the appearance of the fields and of the trees and shrubs since the showers began. On the sward Nature has been spreading her green tints with a lavish hand, — the willows have hung out their golden plumes, and are now putting on a green mantle, and everywhere the buds have been swelling and unfolding, so that the woods and shrubberies have become more dense and richer in colour. A writer in the "London Spectator" has told very daintily the story of the coming of the buds and blossoms of trees as they are seen in old England, and says that to know them aright there, one must begin to observe them from the first day of the new year. And I remember that White of Selborne finds some of the spring flowers even in December. In our climate they are not so enterprising, and I am inclined to think that we enjoy them the more at their coming, because we have had such a long period when life seemed wholly to have passed from the fields and woods.

I am tempted to quote here some verses of my own, published a good many years ago in another place; they were written for children — but are we not all children in the spring?

Glorious sunshine flooding the earth
   Richly with golden showers,
Filling our hearts with gladness and mirth,
   Bringing the birds and flowers;
Joy giving sunshine, happy are we
In the new life that comes from thee!

Softly the raindrops, falling in showers,
   — Each like a tiny ball!
Bring down unstinted life to the flowers,
   Manna to feed them all!
But see! the sunshine gleaming through,
Showeth in heaven a gate of blue!

Over the fields the grasses are creeping,
   Spreading a velvet screen!
Into the light the blossoms are peeping,
   Sparkling amid the green!
Joy-giving sunshine, happy are we
In the new life that comes from thee!

Hark! 'tis the birds that blithely are singing
  Thanks for the sunny hours!
Hark! 'tis the busy bees that are clinging
  Round the just op'ning flowers!
Busy and cheerful workers are ye!
What is your secret, bird and bee?

My neighbours are raking the dry leaves from their lawns, and putting their gardens in order; the road-makers are abroad, spreading soft mould over the driveways, to provide deep mudholes to burrow in when the rain comes; the farmers are busy in the fields preparing for the early crops. And even upon that portion of my "mountain meadow" which I design for a garden and orchard, the plough has been turning the rich soil up to the sun to be aired and sweetened, and what here and there appear to be only arbitrary pitfalls for the unwary are the destined homes of apple and peach and pear and cherry and plum and quince and apricot; and elsewhere, of the elm tree and the white birch.

I wonder if the latter, which so generously clothes the neglected and forgotten fields, and which mounts the rough edge of the deserted gravel pit and plants its little cohorts upon the scarred hillside, will form as graceful a cluster at my bidding, to shut off too long and straight a line of wall, and mark the border of the " home-place."

On the two mornings immediately preceding the rain it was interesting to observe the casts of the earthworms thickly strewn everywhere alongside the paths, and in the pathways themselves, excepting where they had become most solid. Not a worm itself did I see, but there was scarcely a space of five inches anywhere which did not show its little curlicue of fresh soil from beneath. Not more marvellous are the great oaks that grow from the little acorns than are the stupendous changes that are effected upon the surface of the earth by these soft, limp, almost structureless bodies, as Darwin has shown. If any one has a lingering doubt as to the value of individual effort on the part of the ordinary mortal, albeit unconscious effort, and without conscious purpose, let him read the " Earthworms and Vegetable Mould," and be encouraged and consoled.

Undoubtedly it is the exceptional mortals, the thinkers, the giant workers, the strong, the great, that mark epochs and lead the race forward. We see them above others as we look back over the past, like vigorous trees in the forest, like mountain

peaks o'ertopping lesser hills. Mankind
will not forget them. Theirs are

> — the few, the immortal names,
> That were not born to die.

But, as Walt Whitman says, "I sing"
the great unknown, the unnumbered commonplace, who go about their daily tasks
with only the ordinary hopes and fears,
joys and aspirations, wants and woes, virtues and faults, which are the common lot
of the human race. Perhaps even some of
these take themselves quite seriously, and
are fully aware that the machine would go
to pieces if their peg should not be in its
place. But there are numberless others
who believe themselves of no account, and
untold multitudes who think that if only
things were somewhat different, then would
they be able to give this great world the
boost that it needs to send it spinning free
adown the ages, or at least might be able to
give that little aid of which they now feel
incapable.

Courage, good friend! Perhaps " this is
the very place God meant for thee," and out
of it thou wouldst be lost, and it also. Till
thine own acre. A good people is only
made out of good individuals, and the strong

G

and courageous leader can only make a
strong and courageous nation by inspiring
others with his strength and courage. A
stream will not rise higher than its source,
but the fuller the spring, the surer will it
" to higher levels rise."

April 22, 1894.

XV.

When Adam dolve, and Eve span,
Who was then the gentleman?

Did you ever hear an easier conundrum
in your life? The journeyman gardener
who could not guess this at the first attempt,
is not worth his salt.

I have been at it for two days. After
many hours' labour, I am forced this afternoon to confess that it is easier in theory
than in practice. How *can* there be so
many stones in so small a piece of ground?
Why *will* the teeth of the rake catch in
the edge of the sod and turn it up, and
compel me to pull and push and beat it in
order to work out the rich mould, before
the grass can be thrown off upon the border
or left to wither upon the surface? And
why, O why, is it such a labour to get the
kink out of the back, and put some flexibility into the spine once more?

Ah! but when I raise my eyes! There,
before me are the everlasting hills, "from

whence cometh my help," in all their glory
and mystery. And marshalled in mighty
hosts, the great clouds, majestic in form
and magnificent in colour, — sometimes vast
piles of snow, and then deep-toned, sombre
masses, march across the heavens, and anon
the hills are shrouded as with a veil, a sudden gust of wind passes down the valley,
and the rain drops, in serried files, are driven
across the fields. And then the sun breaks
through in the west and dazzles my eyes,
and as my neighbour calls from the adjoining
orchard, I turn eastward, and behold a perfect bow, which, resting at both ends upon
the earth between me and my own woodland,
spans the site of the future home. Shall I,
just for this once, be a trifle superstitious,
and accept the token as a welcome harbin-
ger of the better days that are to be?

APRIL 24, 1894.

XVI.

Das Ewig=Weibliche
Zieht uns hinan.

AMATI, Stradivarius, Guarnerius, — O
sons of Cremona, what subtile spirit
taught you how to shape and tune that
divine instrument which can express as
no other all the aspirations and passions
of the human heart? How its tones twist
and twine around our nerves, until we vi-
brate in unison with its quivering strings,
and are played upon as though we ourselves were the instrument! And she that
handles the bow, how fine her dower, to be
able to evoke at will that mystic charm,
and rule our ear and heart and soul, with
a greater spell than that of the Pied Piper
of Hamelin-town, leading us all a-dancing
through the charmèd aisles of wonderland.
We that have not the gift can do no less
than render just homage where it is due,
not unmingled, perhaps, with a righteous
envy of the power to confer upon others
so great a draught of pleasure. So Viola

played this afternoon, and we all rejoiced. And Brunella, from the cold ivory keys, drew a fitting harmony upon which the lingering and sparkling tones of the violin floated and danced, as upon the crest of the waves. And then from the same keys rippled the tripping melody, and deep and solemn chords responded to an assured and sympathetic touch.

What can one do or say in return for such a pleasure? The scribe ventured only to remark that what was so charming to the hearer must be even a greater delight to the performer. Brunella suggested that the performer suffered sometimes from a consciousness of unsympathetic hearers. But what hearers could fail to be sympathetic under such a spell? Ah! doubtless there are dull ears, and nerves so heavy or so weary, that they fail to respond to the message borne by the pulsing air. And perhaps there may be hearts that are not wholly awake to the finer melodies and harmonies of the universe, to which these tones are but as sound and fury, signifying nothing.

I sometimes wonder why it is that so many people miss the finer shades of meaning in this harmony that we call life, and in very good faith do their little best to convert it into unlovely discord.

The scribe is, as it were, admitted here into the very realm of the Princess Ida, without even the moral support that he might have, were Cyril and Florian with him. The one black sheep amid a flock of ewe lambs this afternoon, he could but shelter himself in a quiet corner, and bless his stars that the lambs were so gentle, and that they were not wolves instead. The man who does not feel abashed in the presence of a pure and noble woman, must himself be very free from tarnish by the world, or he must be very callous.   If she be —

A creature not too bright or good
For human nature's daily food;
For transient sorrows, simple wiles,
Praise, blame, love, kisses, tears and smiles.

 * * * * * *

The reason firm, the temperate will,
Endurance, foresight, strength, and skill;
A perfect woman, nobly planned,
To warn, to comfort, and command:
And yet a spirit still, and bright
With something of angelic light, —

she is surely the crown of life so far as it has yet appeared upon the work-and-play ground of our mother earth.

One must, however, encourage one's self
with the thought that she cannot dispense
with him in the long run, — that there
must be —

                          Everywhere
Two heads in council, two beside the hearth,
Two in the tangled business of the world,
Two in the liberal offices of life,
Two plummets dropped for one to sound the
        abyss
Of science, and the secrets of the mind:
Musician, painter, sculptor, critic, more:
And everywhere the broad and bounteous
        earth
Should bear a double growth of those rare
        souls,
Poets, whose thoughts enrich the blood of the
        world.

Man needs collision of intellect and inter-
change of thought with his fellow-man, and
woman needs to range herself alongside her
sister. But more than all else, each needs
the inspiration that comes from the other.
Their attitude of mind, thought, and feeling
is different : —

For woman is not undeveloped man,
But diverse: could we make her as the man,
Sweet Love were slain: his dearest bond is
        this,

Not like to like, but like in difference:
Yet in the long years liker must they grow;
The man be more of woman, she of man;
He gain in sweetness and in moral height,
Nor lose the wrestling thews that throw the
     world;
She mental breadth, nor fail in childward
     care,
Nor lose the child-like in the larger mind;
Till at the last she set herself to man,
Like perfect music unto noble words;
And so these twain, upon the skirts of Time,
Sit side by side, full summ'd in all their pow-
     ers,
Dispensing harvest, sowing the To-be,
Self-reverent each and reverencing each,
Distinct in individualities,
But like each other ev'n as those who love.

I was struck by Phillis's suggestion in attempting to account for a certain lack of
interest in outward nature and natural
science which appeared to be visible in her
sisters, that their thought and feeling were
by constitution more centred upon the individual human being, and personal relations. Whether this be so, I cannot say,
but certainly there seems to be with them
a definite tendency toward measuring by
the concrete, and ignoring abstract relations and wide affinities and deductions,

as compared with their brothers. And withal, there appears to be a certain intuitive unreasoning clearness of perception in some directions, where all man's careful study occasionally leads him astray, or befogs his vision.

A truce to the absurd discussion as to which is the greater power. In a certain volume which used to be widely read, it is written, "So God created man in his own image, in the image of God created he him ; male and female created he them." And I think that I speak as by authority for one-half of the human race, in saying that out of the smoke of the battle, and out of the dust and heat of the conflict of life, we of the rougher, coarser sort look up for needed refreshment to those who may be a little removed from the worst of this soiling contact ; ask for an occasional breath of a higher, purer air, for a touch that will cool and freshen us, a guiding hand to lead us to the serener heights, whence we can gaze into the infinite distances. And we hope that the time may never come when we cannot repeat, as now we fervently say : —

The ever-womanly leadeth us.

APRIL 23, 1894.

XVII.

A NOT ungentle touch upon the shoulder brought me to myself, and to a realization of the fact that there was an outside world, and I found the conductor standing quietly by my side in that expectant attitude which demands recognition.

I was speeding on my way homeward, with a heavy burden lifted from my mind, but with a leaden weight resting upon my weary eyelids, after long night watches. But how great a contrast in these weights! A glance from the car-window fully awakened me. The spotless heaven smiled back upon the rollicking fruit trees, bursting everywhere into blossom, as into tumultuous laughter; the rich green of the pastures, and the softer shades of the various trees of the wood vied with each other in their effort to refresh the eye; there were the meadows,—

— with daisies pied, and violets blue,

excepting that it was still too early for the daisies, at least for the common white-

weed which we dignify by that name, and
I had to take the buttercups instead; but
there were violets a-plenty, and on the
slopes, the tender blue of that of the bird's-
foot, the loveliest one of all; there were the
moss pinks, the crowsfoot geranium, the
wild azalea, and what-not. How bright it
all was, and how happy they looked!
They toiled not, neither did they spin, and
yet " Solomon, in all his glory, was not arrayed,— was not arrayed, like one of these,
— like one of these." It seemed as if
work were needless, and that we, too,
should vegetate only, in a world so full of
life.

But no such immunity from the common lot is needful. What do I say? — no
such immunity is desirable or grateful, except for the moment. It is the weight
upon the heart that crushes. The knowledge of personal wrong-doing is the worst,
or perhaps the best, in that it brings with
it its own antidote, in the healthful im-
pulse, but next to this, and in a certain
sense the worst of all, is the fact of being
cruelly misconceived and misjudged. Ah!
this is the burden which we feel cannot be
borne, the wrong for which there appears
no remedy, the damned spot which seems

as though it will not out. The heavens grow black, and the waters of the river of life run muddy and sullen. How horrible it all is, — the taint that spreads as a drop of oil upon the face of the waters, until every point we touch is mastered by it, but in how different a fashion!

When, however, the hideous charm is broken, ah! then comes the light! As now the sunlight gleaming through the tender gray green leaves, dancing upon the blades of grass, flashing from the ripples upon the water, sparkling in the blue of the sky; while the brooks murmur and the birds carol as though they were but an embodied joy.

MAY 10, 1894.

XVIII.

WHEN I said that it was a great bore, Phollis remarked in that exasperating way that some young women have of dulling the fine points made by their elders, for whose gray beards and bald pates they should have more respect, that I "must have got that off before, it came so easy." I was speaking of the big hole which I own upon the hillside. I never owned so long a hole before in all my life, and now I cannot take it away with me and make it of any service.

The fact is that workmen have set up a steam engine with other appropriate paraphernalia upon my building site, and for a week past they have been drilling away with a very blunt chisel in search for water. They tell me they have already gone down about seventy-two feet, and have as yet secured a very inadequate supply of that useful commodity. They tell me also that they are on hard pan, and this makes me feel at home, so many of us have been situated in the same way for the past year. And it also has a familiar sound when they add that they do not know how long this condition of affairs may continue.

I looked into the hole, which they have lined with an iron pipe about six inches in diameter, and a very black hole it is, and far on the road toward Calcutta. We all supposed that we should strike rock within a few feet from the surface, and find a suitable supply of water shortly after. But fortune did not favour us, and now I am tied, as it were, to the interior of the earth by a mysterious channel. It is a precious possession. Nobody else in the neighbourhood owns such a hole, and though I sometimes hear of depredations in the village or on the surrounding farms, fruit taken or potatoes dug, or, as, alas! in a recent case, even a horse stolen, I am not afraid of any one pulling this up and carrying it off. It is one thing which I shall be able to keep, and I shall make the most of it.

And now I am going to let out a little secret, which will betray my own ignorance. When I had written that word "paraphernalia" a little way back, it being a rather formidable word, I did as I often do in such cases, — I referred to a small dictionary to make sure that my spelling was correct. I used the small dictionary to save time, notwithstanding that long experience should have taught me that I always have to refer to the larger work before I get through.

Well, I referred to a certain "Pocket Dictionary of the English Language" which has in times past been the cause of much of this sort of trouble, and read, to my dismay, this definition : " Paraphernalia, goods of a wife beyond her dower." A pretty mess I had made of it. Let us see how the phrase runs with the substitution : " A steam engine with other appropriate goods of a wife beyond her dower." Woe is me ! Would any one have supposed in advance that a steam engine should naturally be classed among the appropriate goods of a wife beyond her dower? This opens a large field for speculation, and points to the great extension and importance of the manufacturing era, but also to an extension of the scope of woman's activities. A steam engine would doubtless, in certain emergencies, be a good thing to have in the family, but it has its disadvantages. Phollis told me this afternoon that my bluff rock had been her favourite place of resort for study and quiet reading, but that during the past week she

had been driven from it by the dull and
monotonous thud, thud of the engine. And
I quite shared in her feeling. We do not
desire to shirk labour here, but it is hand
labour and head labour and heart labour
that is to our liking, and naught that reminds us strongly of the great hives of industry which we have left behind us.

And what of those hives? I do not know
whether it is particularly profitable to speculate about the effect of inevitable and un-
avoidable conditions, or relations which
must be lived through. I am inclined to
think, though, that there are certain advantages to be derived from sometimes trying
to get them into proper perspective, and
from picturing to ourselves their causes and
consequences, their necessity and value or
uselessness, their transitoriness or permanence.

When Hero of Alexandria constructed
his æolipile or James Watt his workable
steam engine, how little either of them
thought that he was dealing with an agency
which should not only transform the world,
but should transform the race also! Think,
if you can, of what the world would be to-
day had the steam engine never been in-
vented. No communication between place

and place excepting by row-boat or sailing
vessel on the water, or by animal-power
or on foot on the land; no stupendous dis-
emboweling of the earth for the fuel stored
therein by the sun in ages past, or for
the metals, lead and iron and zinc, copper
and silver and gold; no spanning of mighty
rivers by great bridges; no vast workshops,
swarming with hundreds and thousands of
men and women, gathered at the call of immense machines, whose servants they become, to make millions of copies of a single
pattern, and often of such a pattern as was
never seen on any mount of vision; and
to work, mind upon mind, in a narrow
circle, on the one side increasing and developing mental action, and on the other
limiting, deforming, twisting it, and cramping the individual into the pattern of the
class.

I have particularly in mind just now the
two points to which I have last alluded:
The flooding of the world with countless
copies of articles exactly similar, for whose
form and character their putative makers
have practically no thought or responsibility; and the effect upon these makers of
their herding together. In both respects
the bad and the good are inextricably min-

gled. You can indicate them, but you cannot disentangle them. In the first instance,
possessions have become democratized. The
convenience or the ornament, which once
was only for the select few, or even not for
these, but non-existent, is strewn broadcast
among the multitude, — sold for a song.
But alas! it has lost its soul. No loving,
thoughtful care goes into it; it has no per-
sonality; it has descended, as from a man
to a manikin.

And the workers, what of them? From
the free air, under the broad light of heaven,
they have been drawn into these immense
caravansaries, where their ears buzz with
the whirr, their nerves tremble with the jar,
their nostrils are filled with the mixed efflu-
via of many things which are not nice; to
perform a certain act over and over and
over and over again, plodding through a
tread-mill life; meeting hour after hour,
and day after day, and week after week,
and month after month, with others struggling under like limitations; forced to hear
and parry or accept ideas, and therefore
forced to think, but shut in one eternal
round, with the little of life they see visible as through a distorting lens; how is it
possible that the world should be to them

as it is to those who view it as free individuals out in God's sunshine? Is it strange that all sorts of exploded theories, chimerical schemes, and absurd conceptions of "natural rights" and millennial possibilities should find in such congregations a congenial soil, and that we are from time to time confronted with a problem which it seems impossible to solve: how to clarify this vision, to couch the suffering eyes before it is too late, and the incurable disaster falls upon us? The wonder under these conditions is, I think, that sanity continues to be the rule and has not become the exception, and that somehow there is in the individual a sufficient repulsive power to enable him or her for the most part to resist what would seem to be the inevitable consequences of the position.

But these reflections cause one to pray for some loop-hole through which humanity may creep into a freer air, where the soul can be regained. And I sometimes wonder whether the relief which we seek may not yet be found in the age of electricity, which is following upon the heels of the age of steam. May it not be that the time is coming, and even not far in the distant future, when through storage battery or in some other way the skilled workman may obtain the added power which he now needs, and have it brought to his own dwelling, and thus be enabled to retire " far from the madding crowd," and by personal thought and individual touch impress upon the thing which he creates that character and merit which will conquer for it a place in the affection and in the markets of the world? Let us hope so.

But where was I ? As I live, looking out the meaning of the word paraphernalia in the dictionary. Come, come — no more trifling with this little affair ; let us see what the " Century " has to tell us. Ah ! here it is ; number three will save me, but only as by fire ; " miscellaneous possessions," and I will positively refuse to pay any attention whatever to the rest of the sentence, "as the numerous conveniences of a traveller, small decorative objects, and the like."

MAY 11, 1891.

XIX.

" Look here, upon this picture."

Is it possible that I have permitted seven months to pass without a second visit to Rattlesnake Mountain ? Even so ; and again a stiff breeze is blowing, but laden now with the odours of spring, and full of the promise of the summer days. As we climb the mountain side, Phollis and I, we are greeted now and again by the fragrance of apple blossoms, by the spicy breath of the cedars, exhaling their rich aroma at the solicitation of the warm sun, by the mint which we crush beneath our feet, by the thousand mingled perfumes of tree and shrub and herb which surround us, and of the earth from which they spring, with its carpet of dried leaves.

The notes of many birds come to us through the branches, and we see them fluttering from tree to tree, occasionally showing a bright wing sparkling in a slant sunbeam. Song-sparrow, Maryland yellow

throat, wood robin, redstart, oriole, gros-
beak, thrush — how I wish I knew them
all, and the meaning of their joyous calls!
It scarcely seems as if it would require the
intervention of the cruel uncle to induce us
to lie upon this warm sun-flecked slope, and
be overspread with a leafy counterpane.
But I hardly think that our red-breasted
thrush, masquerading as robin redbreast, as
the whiteweed in its turn does as the

> Wee, modest, crimson tipped flow'r,

is really fully aware how

> Robin redbreast piously
> Did cover them with leaves,

and, just possibly, even now we might run
the risk of a late frost. But how good it is
here!

> Under the greenwood tree
> Who loves to lie with me,
> And turn his merry note
> Unto the sweet bird's throat —
> Come hither, come hither, come hither!
> Here shall he see
> No enemy
> But winter and rough weather.
>
> Who doth ambition shun
> And loves to live i' the sun,

> Seeking the food he eats
> And pleased with what he gets —
> Come hither, come hither, come hither !
> Here shall he see
> No enemy
> But winter and rough weather.

We commit ourselves to the uncertainties of an unknown path which opportunely presents itself, and plunge into the intricacies of the wood. The trees and shrubs are all in leaf, but the leaves — like Little Buttercup — are young and tender, inviting to reckless experiment with teeth and palate, —

> Seeking the food he eats
> And pleased with what he gets, —

that we may be prepared, if peradventure we be lost in the wood, and forced to seek sustenance from sources hitherto untried. I do not advise too free an indulgence in this sort of investigation, however, by those who have not already some knowledge of the organic world in its unsophisticated indigenous forms. But there may be great possibilities here. Did not Lorelei teach us on Cape Cod last summer that the limpets upon the shore were dainties to be prized, and did I not seriously meditate housing

myself in a cabin within sight of the surf,
and, luxuriating upon this delicious diet,
loafing and inviting my soul on the beach
throughout the long summer days?   As I
think of it, memory brings before me the
stretch of yellow grey shore with the rip-
pling edge of the water gently lapping the
sand at my feet as the tide turns, with here
and there protruding the gaunt ribs of a
wrecked coaster, covered with barnacles,
and with waving streamers of seaweed.

> Oh, is it weed, or fish, or floating hair ? —
>   A tress o' golden hair,
>   O' drownèd maiden's hair,
>   Above the nets at sea ?

Behind me is the crumbling bank with its
ragged edge of roots and overhanging grass,
and with the pitch-pines and scrub-oaks
clinging for dear life to the top of the bluff,
while away, away in front stretch the shal-
low waters toward Martha's Vineyard and
Nantucket, which perchance are just lifted
by the mirage upon the edge of the distant
horizon.

And just here a blundering, crooked
branch of witch-hazel stretches across the
path, and we are again on Rattlesnake
Mountain, in the aisles of the merry green-

wood, where many of the young leaves are yet so small as to permit the eye to penetrate between them into the heart of the forest. And in return, I cut a good forked branch of the witch-hazel to test its traditional virtues, and trim it to the satisfaction of my companion. Is it to be wondered at, that in the hands of the seeress thus equipped, it shortly pointed toward the centre of the earth, upon a spot beneath which doubtless pulses a restless spring, eager to be released? Far be it from us to suggest a distrust of such an indication, by trying to pry into the heart of Nature's secrets. Much more proper was it to show our loyalty by erecting upon the spot a monument consisting of the wand itself.

The convenient path winds around the side of the hill, here a scarcely marked track, and there deeply gullied by the late winter torrents, but now dry and irregularly strewn with loose stones. At length the bolder rocks come into view upon our right, and leaving the path we climb from headland to headland until we are upon the very summit, with the world of town and city, farm and forest spread at our feet.

The long-wished-for rain has not come, and the last year's leaves are dry, and miles away to the northward a vast cloud of grey smoke from fiercely burning woods rises in puffs high into the air, and spreads itself in gradually attenuated sheets until we trace it thinly in delicate wreaths, far toward the southern horizon. And anon comes to us a whiff of its agreeable odour, a faint apology for the cruel wound the fire is making upon the distant mountain-side.

After viewing the kingdoms of the world and the glory of them, we sit upon the weather-worn rock, which is lined here and there with delicate intersecting ridges of harder material, looking, as Phollis says, like the interlaced markings upon the back of a Brobdignagian hand. And from his capacious pocket, the scribe, playing an ancient and familiar trick, — familiar at least to him, produces an old-fashioned blue and gold volume. How dainty this style seemed to us, six lustrums ago, before the beginning of the flood of handsome and handy books with which the publishers have favoured us in these latter years! And we prize them yet, and this among the best, this book of Clough's, of our poet immigrant of forty years ago, that earnest but restless spirit, whom some loved so much, both those who knew him personally, and those of us who did not, and whom now so few remember. Some things that he wrote they cannot escape knowing: the—

> Say not, the struggle naught availeth,

and

> As ships, becalmed at eve, that lay
>   With canvas drooping, side by side,
> Two towers of sail at dawn of day
>   Are scarce, long leagues apart descried;

and

> Come back, come back! behold with straining mast
> And swelling sail, behold her steaming fast;

ending with the fine

> Come back, come back!
> Back flies the foam; the hoisted flag streams back;
> The long smoke wavers on the homeward track;
> Back fly with winds things which the winds obey:
> The strong ship follows its appointed way.

And some of these things the scribe read aloud to his companion. But there are many more that they ought to know, others of the minor poems, and the " Bothie," and parts of the "Amours de Voyage," and "Dipsychus." There is a resonance, a lilt in his language, as in the accumulation of Scotch names in

Wherefore in Badenoch then, far away, in
    Lochaber, Lochiel. in
Knoydart, Moydart, Morrer, Ardgower, and
    Ardnamurchan,

but there is more than the resonance and the lilting. And as the scribe reads the familiar words, again the mountain fades away, and he is a boy once more, reading aloud on a long carriage journey "The Bothie of Toper-na-Fuosich," as it was first called, his heart even then filled and swelling with its music, and its suggestions of another and far different world, and a life covered with the glamour of romance.

MAY 17, 1894.

XX.

" — and on this."

Last evening we gathered in the village hall, and La Signora Alba beguiled our ears with old Volkslieder ; with pure tone and sympathetic touch, interpreting alike the lover's appeal, the exile's regret at parting, and the rich phrases of the chorale. And then we went out into the night, and found the path flecked with moonbeams, and each wished to see the other safe at home, and we reached the end of the village street ere it seemed time to turn and retrace our steps. And a tiny nerve fibre somewhere under the scribe's epidermis vibrated pleasantly when Phillis said that certain sketches by an unknown writer seemed fated to make her cheerful in spite of herself.

Left alone in the night, I remembered that I wished to mark the true meridian upon my building site, so that the cottage may be set at the proper angle. It is to face exactly toward the northwest, partly because the hill slopes in that direction, and partly that the sun, which dominates our life, may at some time on every bright day send its purifying rays into each of its rooms. If the wild flowers of the field need the caressing touch of the sunlight, how much more do we, of the larger and fuller, if not nobler and more beautiful growth !

So I mounted the hill, and climbed the bars into the meadow. (I do not readily become accustomed to this term as applied to elevated grounds and hillsides. In the Middle States I have only heard it used in relation to valley lands.) Notwithstanding the drought, the grass is well grown, but I found it perfectly dry, though the night was not cloudy. I remember that a certain writer whose interesting essays I have recently read, apparently speaking with authority, tells us that the dew ascends from the soil, and in part is exuded directly by the grass and other plants. If this be true, — and the ninth edition of the Encyclopedia Britannica does not confirm it, — I do not wonder that the grass was not wet. All the soil in holes dug to-day in which to plant some belated fruit and shade trees, was found to be dry and crumbling.

My scheme contemplated an observation of the pole star, which was visible, but only dimly, because of the moonlight, and because the atmosphere was full of what appeared to be a dry haze, presumably smoke and dust. I chose this plan because the variation of the needle here is considerable and uncertain, and near these trap ledges the compass is apt to be a false and treacherous guide.

I first drove a slender stake into the ground, and then taking another a few feet to the southward of it, and humbling myself with my eye close to mother earth, took repeated observations until I had satisfied myself that I had secured a range as accurate as possible. Then I drove in my second stake firmly also, and the thing was done.

From the woodland along the ledge, sounded the melancholy note of the whippoor-will; from a distant kennel came the bark of an uneasy dog; lamps shone from windows here and there; and all the valley was suffused with the soft light of the moon, in which every object finally disappeared in a nebulous haze. It was the first time that I had stood at this hour upon the spot with which the future is to make me

so familiar in all its phases.   At such a
place, at such a time, one has a curiously
mingled sense of solitude and companionship.   No one was near me; no one knew
where I was, — perhaps no one greatly
cared : —

I heard the trailing garments of the Night
    Sweep through her marble halls !
I saw her sable skirts all fringed with light
    From the celestial walls !
I felt her presence, by its spell of might,
    Stoop o'er me from above ;
The calm, majestic presence of the Night,
    As of the one I love.

But before and below me, here and there,
twinkled the home stars, around which were
gathered father and mother, sister and
brother — yes and doubtless

          — a dearer one
       Still, and a nearer one
       Yet than all other.

Might I not venture to claim a part in all
this home-life, and, resting upon my solitary
terrace, drop a gentle thought to mingle
with, perhaps to fructify and stimulate the
lives which it should touch ?

MAY 17, 1894.

I

XXI.

Sweet day, so cool, so calm, so bright,
The bridal of the earth and sky.

It has been absolutely superb. The long storm with which the drought closed has finally passed away, and it has left us with the atmosphere washed clean, but with great floating masses of cloud, lagging, not by any means superfluous, upon the stage, but so as to present to us every variety of beauty that we could desire.

I have spent nearly the whole day, sitting in the shade of my own ash tree, reading and receiving sundry callers, and listening to the birds of all sorts and sizes, as merry as grigs; and anon looking across the field of the cloth of gold made by the buttercups, upon the valley and the distant hills, where the shadows of the slowly moving clouds produced an ever-varying play of light that was infinitely beautiful.

And I have been travelling in delightful familiar paths, and steeping myself in the

joys of the past, tempered by that regret
which must now always endure, as I have
read the manuscript pages of the story of
the life of our Bayard, our knight without
fear and without reproach, Curtis, whom,
alas! we shall see no more on this earth
forever. What joy he would have taken in
this day and in this spot! There were no
need of Titbottom's spectacles, and the
finest castles in Spain could not rank as real
estate at a higher value than the invisible
cottage outlined by cords, and surrounded
by rough boarding here at my side, which
he would so gladly have seen complete and
tenanted.

How can it be possible that any one who
was so fortunate as to be baptized with the
holy chrism of the love and confidence of
this sweet and tender spirit, should ever
thereafter do an unworthy thing or think
an unworthy thought! Alas! that it should
be so! As I read, and the years of the
past are recalled, I again become conscious
of the noble presence, I feel once more the
touch of the gentle hand, I see the tender,
affectionate look in the true eye, and I hear
the musical voice which is now silent for-
evermore. Ah! me! it is worth having
lived to have had such a friend; and how

wide and rich was his capacity for friend-
ship!

Last week it was my fortune to attend
a meeting at the club of those who are
charged with the duty of preparing some
appropriate memorial which shall testify to
coming generations of the supreme regard
in which he is held by many of the best of
this. There was the ex-mayor, who is rapidly building a somnolent college into a
great university ; there was the poet-editor
who lately sang of the blossoming and the
evanishment of the great White City ; there
was the genial essayist, my neighbour — still
going with good cheer on his little journey
in the world ; there was the representative
of the time-honoured publishing house of the
Cheerible brothers ; there was the barrister
by whom rogues most dread to be cross-
examined, the doctor for whom the profes-
sion does not afford a field broad enough
for his energies, the painter who knows
how to catch the very spirit of the New
England village, and the general who can
hold an audience hanging upon his word,
and who can tell, because he saw it with
his own eyes, how his great chief received
the sword of Lee under the tree at Appo-
mattox. And there were the best of words

from the wise and shrewd bishop who can
drive in double harness in perfect amicable-
ness such curiously mismated clerical
steeds, and over the vibrating wire came
the voice of our good friend who gives me
the privilege that I have enjoyed to-day.
It was a noteworthy company, and testified,
as it has been testified in many ways, to the
strong and vital influence which he of whom
I write, whether in the field of political
conflict, upon the rostrum, at the desk, in
the Easy Chair, or by the fireside, has exer-
cised upon the best of his generation.

As I turn over these pages, I strike upon
passages which bring up vividly picture
after picture. As this, in a letter written
on the 20th of April, 1861 : "This day in
New York has been beyond description,
and remember, if we lose Washington to-
night or to-morrow, as we probably shall,
we have *taken New York.*" Do you realize that in that crisis it really seemed that
Washington must go, and that it is most
singular that it did not ? It was completely
at the mercy of the southern troops. In
April, 1892, while a party of us were on
our way to Baltimore, our friend the general — not the general of whom I spoke a
moment ago — told us the story of how he

reached Washington by stealth in those days of suspense, bearing dispatches which conveyed to the President and the cabinet from the governor of this state of ours, the first news which they received of the rising in the North, — the good news that the boys had begun that great march which was to last four weary years. The enemy commanded the city, and must have failed to occupy it simply because they did not know that they had but to march in and take possession. And then a few hours, and the news came that the troops were near by, and our friend was told to watch the flagstaff upon the Senate end of the capitol, because the flag would be displayed therefrom the instant the boys came in sight. And then a few moments more of suspense, and behold the flag was flung to the breeze, and Washington was saved.

Or this fragment from a letter of April 4, 1865: "I thought of you all the day yesterday as the news of the crowning mercy came rolling in. The merchants and brokers in Wall street came out of their dens and sang 'Old Hundred' and 'John Brown.'" Do I not remember it as though it were yesterday? What an inexpressible joy there was in the air, and how we all tried to do what we could to express it! The leaders stood in the great dark colonnade of the custom-house, but the day was bright, and our hearts were full; the street was crowded as far as one could see, and we sang and sang, until we were all hoarse. How dark the cloud had been, and how long and dreary the days; but now the cloud was lifted, the end had come!

And I see another picture. Peace had lasted for almost a generation, and we, a non-combatant body-guard, accompanied the orator on his way to deliver the address on the twenty-fifth anniversary of the battle of Gettysburg, in July, 1888. Of the dozen who formed the party then, alas! already the chief and three others have joined the majority. But then were three perfect days, in which Walter Howe, who was to leave us in his prime, catered for the party as though he had been to the manner born. Pearson told us of the trials which encompass the man who undertakes to do his simple duty in a great office, and Barlow showed us where he fought, bled, and almost died in the good cause. And the leader hallowed us all by his presence, and focussed in himself the interests and the aspirations of all. And we explored the wildnesses of the Devil's Den, and became appropriately confused between Seminary Hill and Cemetery Hill, and looked upon the sea of faces from the North and from the South, and listened to the silver tones of the orator of the day at the gathering place in the national cemetery, and to the manly words of Longstreet and of Gordon, who had been leaders in the invading army.

And again: I see the streets of the Monumental city in April, 1892, and then a great company gathered around a festal board. And as the leader rises to speak, so rise also all the members of the company, with cheer upon cheer, and with eyes moist with the dew that comes to men only when the heart is touched. And before me now lies the pencilled draft which so inadequately recalls that speech as it was delivered, that choicest of after-dinner speeches. And I hear him conclude: "Whatever may become of us, fellow pioneers, I say to you as Latimer said to Ridley at the stake: 'Be of good cheer, Brother Ridley, for we shall this day light such a candle in England as shall never be put out.' If I were to propose a legend for the league, I should turn again to the episcopate, and take the reputed words of the most famous of English church-

men, the cardinal who was the great master
of statecraft in his time, whom Shakespeare
re-created for the English-speaking race,
'Corruption wins not more than honesty.'

"It is the spring of the year, and it is the
springtime of reform. It is not the harvest, but it is the sowing. The blossoms
that open in this soft spring air are flowers
only, not yet fruit. But they are promises
of the summer, and the fruit is sure. They
are voluntary pledges of nature, and in its
benign administration in which seed-time
and harvest never fail, those pledges will
be completely fulfilled. The little twig of
Magna Charta has become the wide-spread-
ing tree of English liberty. Our bud of
reform will become a system of honester
politics."

And then as we rumbled through the otherwise silent streets, he and I, on the way to
our temporary abiding place in the hospitable mansion of our good friend, whose
countenance so strongly reminds us of the
First Consul — as well it may, — the stars
beaming and the moon flooding our path
with its limpid light, softened and touched
and exhilarated by the loyalty, the affection,
the generous emotion which had been shown
him on every hand, and with the knowledge

that the good cause, the purification of the public service and of methods of administration, was moving steadily forward, — though never so full of life, it seemed as though he might have sung his "nunc dimittis." And is it any wonder that we felt it hard, even at that small hour, to seek our couches ? —

> — the best of all ways
> To lengthen our days,
> Is to steal a few hours from the night, my
>   dear.

Tom Moore's lines never came more appropriately than as he quoted them then, looking out upon the night; but indeed the night, that night of nights, seemed speeding all too soon.

MAY 27, 1894.

XXII.

The boring of the well was stopped at a depth of seventy-eight feet, a tiny stream from some mysterious source having been intercepted, which promises an ample supply for all time to come. And yesterday the spade was put into the ground, and now the gash then made in the fresh green turf has grown into a long and broad rectangular hole, with certain projections, in which the cottage is to be planted. It is to be set upon the hardpan, and firmly adjusted to the hillside and tied to the soil by the roots of embracing vines, thus becoming by graft a permanent part of the field, as it is to be hoped that the life which it will enshrine may become a permanent part of the life of this village.

In no respect, perhaps, is our condition at so great a disadvantage when contrasted with that of the old world, as in the lack of ancestral homes. We are continually on the move. We are always new. We never let our roots have time enough to become attached to the soil, but are incessantly tearing them up and breaking off all the delicate fibres through which they should drink in the life needed to sustain us for fine social uses. We not only " have no continuing city " here, — which would not be so bad, since we have no city which as a whole is yet worthy of continuance, — but we have no continuing country, either. We are like the people at Mt. Desert ; some of us are cottagers, and some of us are boarders, and some of us are hauled mealers, and some are only mealers.

Perhaps this is the most inappropriate place in the country in which to indulge such reflections, for in this village there is a certain permanence, and one finds around him owners of one or other of nearly all the names which appear upon the records of two hundred and fifty years ago. This is one of the great attractions of the village, and it is much to be hoped that if it should gradually lose this distinction of permanence it will only be through the increase in that quality on the part of other localities. For I am persuaded, not that immovability is a supreme virtue, but that a vital attachment between a family and its environment is a good thing. And this refers both to the relation between the family and the community, and to the relation between the family and its home. It is a good thing to be born, to live, and to die in the same house; to have associations with every nook and cranny, to be in touch with every turn and corner; to have associations of childhood and of youth, of manhood or womanhood and of old age. And it is a good thing to have generation follow generation, or if fate may not be so kind, to have still a continuous family-life by some sort of incorporation or adoption, which may go on from age to age.

I care not whether it be objective or simply subjective, the kindred feeling which grows strong between the animate tenant and the inanimate domicile, its stones, its beams, and its projecting roof; it is just as real and just as true. Even in the great city hive, with its numberless cells, our own particular cell soon seems to receive us with a friendly welcome all its own. But this is merely a proof of the strength of an imperious instinct. It is out under the blue heaven, where there are trees and grassy fields, where a house has four sides, and all open to the winds and the seasons; where there are individual stepping-stones

worn by the outgoing and incoming of generations ; where there is a fireside at which
have been whispered tender vows, where
merry peals of laughter have been heard,
and jest and roundelay ; where hearts have
bled and heads have been bowed in sorrow ; it is only here that human life seems to
become really and truly a settled and integral and organic part of the world life.

MAY 30, 1891.

XXIII.

IT set me thinking. What was it? Why, the other evening in the cloister, we had a little concert by the Kneisel quartet; it was this which set me thinking.

In the first place, I wondered whether it were possible that those whose ears are trained to all the niceties of musical composition and expression, whose knowledge makes that of the mere layman seem as nothingness, could have an enjoyment in this wealth of sound in proportion to their knowledge. I confess that I found myself a little inclined to skepticism. I remembered the princess who tossed and tossed upon her bed, because of the rose-leaf hidden beneath — how many mattresses was it? Extreme delicacy and sensibility bring with them a certain penalty, and possibly, after all, we of the grosser natures have our compensation, and in the long run drink a deeper draught of life. I will not push the suggestion, for I am not by any means sure that it is true. The supreme

moments pay for ages of commonplace and
of suffering. Against those who hold that
the days of childhood are one's happiest
days, I shall always boldly contend. It is
not possible. Perhaps it may appear so
from the outside, and upon a superficial
view. The accumulating years bring sorrow in their train, pain and deep distress,
and desolation. But they bring also the
wider and fuller capacity for enjoyment,
and for most — can I not say, for all ? —
moments, at least, of delight compared with
which the pleasures of a child are as a
glow-worm's tiny spark to the giant search-
light which threw its beam athwart the
sky from the roof of the Hall of the Liberal
Arts.

I can only say that if the enjoyment of
these knowing ones is so much greater
than ours, it is impossible to understand
how they can endure it. It seems as if the
nerves must reach such a tension at a certain point in their vibration that they must
of necessity give way, and the individual
must dissolve into his original elements, as
the Prince Rupert's drop, when the point is
broken, flies into an impalpable powder.

And then I thought of the stages by
which this sensibility has been reached,

of the long journey which our race has travelled, and the races which preceded it, since time began. Modern music and the ear to which it commends itself are but a few hundred years old, but far back of this period, the ear that was not pleased with concord of sweet sounds, was doubtless already fit for treasons, stratagems, and spoils, although the sounds which were sweet then, might not now so seem to us. And farther still in the distance, we should reach the tom-tom and its contemporaries. But this is still in modern times. Away, far, far beyond, the thought is carried, back to the dawn of that which · we call life, to the point where the inorganic (who shall dare to say that it has not life ?) merges indistinguishably and by slow degrees into the organic.

We talk of the five senses, but how many senses there may be we do not know. In this early dawn of which I dream, hearing was not, nor sight, taste was not, nor smell, and feeling was but about to be born.

Have you ever lived with a microscope of high power, watching those infinitesimal vegetable specks, the diatoms, travelling around in the vast waste of the minutest drop of water that you could lift upon the

K

point of a needle, wandering from place to
place, crossing, meeting, and passing on,
each delicately and exquisitely marked
with a myriad lines and dots, every one
according to his kind? Already you are
far from the beginning. You must go back,
far back of these until you reach the verge
of the amorphous, until you can hardly
more than guess that there exists either
form or motion or individuality. You find
at length that which gives evidence of attraction or repulsion at its lowest term, at
a point a thousand ages before anything
that you can predicate as consciousness.
Between this point and the point to which
I called your attention at the opening of
this note, lies the gulf which has been
crossed; this is the journey of life of which
I speak.

Realize it if you can. Try to picture to
yourself this great march of the living universe; the life born in the atom, growing
and spreading and reaching forward, life
added to life, life piled upon life, life ever
richer and fuller and deeper and higher;
touch and taste and smell and sight and
hearing; thought and memory and reflection; imagination and speculation; love
and honour and reverence and devotion.

And ever as the sight grows stronger and
the vision clearer, the horizon widens, and
the inscrutable power which includes, em-
braces, and controls us becomes more in-
timate, more majestic, more absolutely
undefinable, more awe-inspiring, —

> a sense sublime
> Of something far more deeply interfused,
> Whose dwelling in the light of setting suns,
> And the round ocean and the living air,
> And the blue sky, and in the mind of man:
> A motion and a spirit, that impels
> All thinking things, all objects of all thought,
> And rolls through all things.

JUNE 6, 1894.

XXIV.

"DOUBTLESS God could have made a better berry, but doubtless God never did." Thus genial Izaak Walton quotes Dr. Boteler concerning the strawberry. Upon the hill-top and in the meadow, the ripe, wild berries are now sparkling. a vivid red amid the green in the occasional sunshine, staining the dainty fingers of the picker, and telling tales upon the rosy lip even though the toll be light. This afternoon I found them so plentiful over a considerable space, that I could not put my foot down among them without crushing some. These wild berries are small, but they have a pleasant flavour of freedom about them. I wonder whether this would flee as soon as we tried to tame them ?

I see that it is said that our present cultivated berries are descended from a Chili strawberry, this having succeeded an earlier form developed from the Virginia berry. Perhaps it might not be amiss to take a new start. The markets of our

great cities call for such enormous supplies
of fruit, that they must be brought from
vast distances, and as a consequence those
varieties are encouraged which will bear
preservation and transportation. In soft
fruits, therefore, especially strawberries and
peaches, there is a tendency to sacrifice
flavour and delicacy for these qualities of
permanence, until Dr. Boteler, or Butler,
might not be able always to recognize the
berry that he loved.

One of my neighbours called upon me yesterday to accompany her over the hill to
investigate a shrub or small tree which had
aroused her curiosity. It proved to be the
prickly ash or toothache tree, of which I
have many in my wood, a tree worth cul-
tivating, especially on account of its bright
berries. This particular specimen showed
a peculiarity which I have not noticed in
others, a tendency in some of the branches
to flatten at the joints or intersections, and
to form ridges something like a cock's-comb.
The books do not seem to refer to this. I
shall have to examine further to determine
whether it is constitutional, simply an
idiosyncrasy, or due to insect or fungoid
agency. The two latter causes of peculiar
vegetable growth are so multifarious in

their forms of working, and withal so marvellous, that the specialist alone can make much headway in their investigation.

We saw in the same locality a specimen of the viburnum opulus or bush-cranberry, which I am glad to discover in my neighbourhood. It was quite new to me when I found it last summer, up in the neighbourhood of "Sky farm" and Mt. Everett, its profusion of richly coloured berries putting to shame the tame prim crudities of the mountain ash. I thought it much more attractive than its cultivated descendant, the guelder rose or snowball of our gardens.

The heavy and frequent rains which followed the brief drought have produced a great development in the leafage, and I think that I never saw the forest more dense or luxuriant. The scaffolding of the hills is concealed, and only here and there can we now trace from a distance the lines of crag. Upon the fields we find a succession of colours, pleasant to look upon, though not always gratifying to the farmer. At first I thought that I was to have a beautifully uniform crop of hay, — the turf seemed so green and smooth. Then it became sprinkled here and there with quaker ladies or bluets, as if some careless body had been trying to cover the sky with a coat of whitewash, with just a tint of blue in it, and had allowed the colour from his brush to spatter all over the carpet. After this came the buttercups, and made a very sea of gold, which I fear as a circulating medium would prove almost as worthless as the silver which our western friends desire us to accept, though certainly much more beautiful. And now we have the ox-eye daisy, known by those upon whom is imposed the duty of trying to exterminate it as the whiteweed, but christened by Linnæus with the imposing name of chrysanthemum leucanthemum. Myriads and myriads of the starry disks look up into the sky to see their fellows of the firmament. Phollis says that they are small and degenerate and not worthy representatives of the race, but I know better. And besides, I am glad that they are small; such are the best kind.

But as I look over the field I seem to hear the grass saying in the popular slang: " Where do I come in ? " My neighbour over the way has purchased my crop of hay in advance, and I hope that he may find it. I know one spot where it is lush and high, and here among the long thick green leaves, you may discover the most glorious heads of the red clover that you ever saw, full of honey, too, which I envy the bees. And there comes a great buzzer who has found the store, and means to contest with us the possession of the field. And I am sure that he is armed for the fray, and that courtesy requires that I should speed the parting guest, the stranger within my gates, who carries away some of my berries and a bit of my heart as well, and so plucking a handful of the showy heads I gracefully retire from the contest without breaking a lance.

And what if we linger at the bars, while I try in vain to parry, to find fitting defence and reply to the verbal arrows which are shot at me? One must sometimes — to himself only, mind you — admit defeat, and learn to find a wholesome enjoyment in the same.

JUNE 7, 1894.

XXV.

"God tempers the wind to the shorn lamb." Though it was Laurence Sterne that wrote it, I am sure that no indignity has been done the Bible by its common attribution to that source, and it is no less truly descriptive of the fact than if it were to be found upon the pages of the holiest of books. For though his ways are said not to be as our ways and his thoughts not to be as our thoughts, and though the sun rises upon the evil and upon the good, and the rain falls upon the just and the unjust alike, nevertheless the winds are tempered in a very real fashion. For what matters it how biting the blast, if we do not feel it? And is it not the universal human experience that how sore soever troubles may be, the neck gradually becomes accustomed to the yoke, the new conditions are accepted as a part of the natural order, and we gradually find ourselves adjusted to them? Even though at first it seems as if all the sweetness had gone out of life, as if in future, summer and winter, seed-time and harvest, would be for us as if they were not, at length we see the sunlight again, we hear the lark sing, we inhale the fragrance of the rose ; as it was in the beginning, we look upon creation, and behold it is very good.

The adjustment takes a little time ; we have to become accustomed to the new conditions ; new channels must be opened ; but the fact that stunned us in the morning — by the evening we have always known it. If our fortunes have suddenly changed, and all seems lost, wait but a few hours and we are busy with new devices, seeking out new combinations, finding hope where hope there seemed none.

I remember that at one time in my boyhood I was engaged in an office in the neighbourhood of a great town clock — it was that of Independence Hall in Philadelphia. The peals of the bell striking the hour seemed loud enough to wake the dead. But after a while it became a thing of custom. I would say to myself, " I will look at my watch and compare it when the clock strikes twelve," and then I would go on with my writing, and some time later suddenly remember and take out my watch and find that the great bell must have rung out its twelve heavy strokes a half-hour before, yet the accustomed nerve of sense had conveyed no message to the brain.

Sometimes the friction endures, and the note of pain reaches the bystander after many days, months, or years. I have been sitting in the wood, and as the wind swayed the branches I would hear the appeal of some dryad among them, moaning in her pain. Sometimes it has required quite a long search to discover the sufferer, but at length it would be found, a branch which year after year had borne the burden of another, ever becoming heavier and more insistent as the years rolled on, and grinding its way into the vital substance. And then again I have found instances where as time had passed the two had become incorporate, and the wood nymph had escaped her torture by appropriating her burden as an integral part of her substance.

It is well when strength can thus be conquered from calamity. Each time Antæus was thrown to the ground, his vigour was increased; contact with mother earth gave strength to her child. So it should be always, and so, I fondly hope, it usually is.

But when I began, I was thinking more

particularly of the beneficence of the arrangement by which that which at first is the cause of much perplexity, of great distress, of sore grief, soon becomes diluted as it were, mixed with other ingredients, and even before any solution is found, any issue is discovered, ceases to be the terrible thing it was in the beginning. Sometimes this is doubtless simply because the tired brain becomes numbed, and the nerves refuse any longer to bear so acute a current. But this in itself is a part, and a large part of the "tempering" of which I spoke. The wind bloweth where it listeth, and it still beats about the devoted head; but the blast is silent, or as on the harp of Æolus, the shriek of agony dies away in a plaintive murmur.

JUNE 10, 1894.

XXVI.

PHOLLIS made a little exclamation and stopped me as I was about to step upon a mottled brown snake, which lay in a slightly waving line across the middle of the sandy wood-road. The compensating curve of its body was really very graceful, but it was difficult to conjure up any emotion of pleasure as we looked at it. It seemed at first perfectly still, but on examining it narrowly the motion of its breathing apparatus could be discovered. I have an invincible repugnance for all snakes, noxious and innocuous alike, which, nevertheless, I try to conquer, and I touched it with a light branch which I had in my hand, to ascertain whether its sluggishness were only assumed. It immediately flattened and hollowed its neck for a length of several inches, and darted out its forked tongue in very vicious fashion. I looked about for a loose stone or heavy stick with which to make a demonstration in force, but meantime the reptile softly glided away among the bushes and was lost.

When I described it to my neighbour afterward, he said that it was probably a red adder, one of the few poisonous serpents of these parts. It was not very red, and may not have been an adder, or a madder as it seems we should properly say, but it was dangerous enough in appearance to be anything of the kind you might name. Possibly it was a copperhead, that unseemly reptile which strikes unexpectedly and without warning, and which a generation ago lent its name to those rebel sympathizers in the North who formed our weakest spot in the war days, and doubtless to many others whom it was cruel injustice to class with these. For when the nation was in dire peril, people did not stop to make nice discriminations, and sometimes conduct which was simply the result of a more delicate conscientiousness or more philosophical apprehension upon the part of the individual, was attributed to a much less worthy cause.

We have not a great many venomous reptiles, and I believe that I never knew a person who had been bitten by one. And yet I have a constant and very lively dread of them, as I have intimated, and I believe that this feeling is largely shared by others.

The snake is perhaps more graceful in its

motions than any other living thing, — even than a kitten, — and yet instead of enjoying these, similar motions in other beings excite in us a certain repulsion, at least poetically, because of this association. Is not this really, in part, at least, a "survival in culture," — a result of the traditional identification of the serpent with the supposed embodiment of the principle of evil?

We are magazines, full of these remnants of the past, which sometimes wear out, but often long endure to colour our opinions and our reasoning, and control our action. Our whole social structure is based upon them, and the effort to effect a sudden revolution is as senseless as anything of which you can conceive. Why is it good form to sell certain things by the ton, but ignoble to sell them by the pound? Why is service in a store or office respectable, and service in a house menial? Why is a certain kind of service paid for at a certain rate, and another service, just as simple, paid for at four times that rate? Why, a thousand things that pass before us every day without attracting our observation, simply because we have always been accustomed to them? We do not know anything more, than that under the interaction of the various forces which have controlled human development, — an infinite variety of forces, — they have worked out so. We may not feel wholly satisfied with the result. We may think that the burdens are borne unequally by different classes and individuals. We may try to modify the existing order. But there is no use in "getting mad" about it; that will not help matters. The pope's bull against the comet was of little service. Canute did not stop the incoming of the tide. The *vis inertiæ* is a mighty power, and you may as well take it into account. Keep your head level. See what is possible, and do that. Do not allow yourself to become a scold, and on the other hand do not permit yourself to be merely as a cork floating upon the top of the wave. Find out if you can in which way the permanent channels lie, whither the current must ultimately run, toward what point the eternal trade winds blow; head your bark thitherward, and pull with all the might that is in you.

But I am afraid that we did not think of all these things as we strolled along that afternoon. It was warm, but fortunately a mantle of cloud covered us with a grateful shade, and when we entered the pine wood we were flooded with the spicy fragrance from the trees. The purple cypripediums long eluded us, but there they were at last, and the lupines, and by the brookside the fleur-de-lis.

And here on the edge of the sandy road is the inconspicuous and unattractive sheep laurel; had our tramp carried us farther away among the hills, we should have found its nobler cousin the mountain laurel, now in its prime, with great white and rosy masses of most lovely blossoms. There upon my chiffonier are some splendid clusters. which have been gradually opening in water during the past six days. Nothing else upon our hillsides is quite so fine as this royal shrub. The native rhododendron is massive but pale. The pink azalea is rich, but not so plentiful or pronounced. The laurel is the prince of the June woods, and holds a royal state. I think that nowhere else will you find it quite equalling the display that it makes around Lake Mohonk, but it bravely holds its own over a vast territory.

Some time ago, when there was considerable talk about a national flower, this was suggested as especially suitable, the leaves, the buds, and the blossoms alike being fine, and peculiarly adapted to effective use in

I.

decorative work. Were it possible to select a "national flower" out of hand, perhaps no more happy choice could be made than this. But what an absurd idea it is! I fear that we are hardly poetic enough as a people to be entitled to a national flower. If we were, we should know that this is a matter to be determined by feeling, by natural growth, by common consent, not by popular vote. In the state of New York a ballot for a state flower was taken among the children of the public schools. The majority voted for the golden-rod. But what golden-rod? I think there are said to be somewhere in the neighbourhood of seventy species, varying in all sorts of ways, and, graceful and beautiful as some of them are, they are not definite and distinctive in flower, but rather attractive masses or sprays.

Let us have a national flower, if you please, and all other good things, when the time comes and we deserve them, but do not let us reach them by way of the factory system. Perhaps it is one of many indications that we are outgrowing our first crude national stage that the question is raised, but we can afford to go slowly until ideas of this kind cease to be novel. Let us resolutely refuse to bury ourselves in the clutter of material things, and I fancy that we shall find our perceptions opening to a flood of impressions which cannot fail to leave a finer stamp upon our spirits and our hearts.

JUNE 12, 1894.

XXVII.

NINETY-TWO in the shade. It was at seventy-eight when I saw it last at night; this morning it was at seventy-three. The cocks were crowing and the hens cackling as usual, the robins, sparrows, and other birds were singing their accustomed matin song; far away in the woods the air was filled with a murmur which did not fully reveal itself, but may have been the warning note of the coming swarm of "seventeen-year locusts," upon the eastern border of which we should find ourselves. As the day waxed older, the mercury climbed higher, and the parched air brought to us no note of comfort. The church-going, or pleasure-going teams (there must be something wrong where the church-going teams are not also in some true sense pleasure-going teams, — wrong in the goers or in the churches) filled the air with a dust so fine from the dry roadways, that much of it floated high into the slightly moving air.

Some of the little ones must have tum-

bled out of bed the wrong end foremost.
So we used to put it, but I suppose that we
shall have to admit that it was only the
extra fever in the blood that caused the
fractious ways which manifested themselves
where all is generally serene. I am sure
that the babies — God bless them ! — do not
know how the endless little shrieks and
fretting wear upon the nerves, themselves
undergoing a sort of disintegration. "Tom
won't give me this," and "Hal won't let
me have that, mamma," and "I don't
want to," and all the negative situations
possible, come to the surface. And then a
little clear laugh or gurgle of delight tells
us that joy has not quite gone out of the
world.

And we all compare notes upon the mo-
mentous subject. "Isn't it hot !" and
"It's going to be hotter than yesterday,"
and "Were you ever in such a hot place
before in your life ?" and "Oh, if we
could only have a shower !" and "Proba-
bilities says that we shall have one this
afternoon," and "That's the worst news
I've heard yet; then we're sure not to have
one." All the familiar phrases come along,
as new as ever.

The hammocks are filled and swinging;

the enormous and abominable metropolitan
Sunday newspapers lie strewn upon the
porch and on the grass, filled to overflow-
ing with things that nobody wants to know,
or ought to want to know, with here and
there a little pure true thought, a breath of
natural life, a lift of imagination, a glimpse
into the ideal.

The scribe had some writing to do, and
he has discovered after not one or two,
but after many experiences, that as the
way in which to resume specie payments
was to resume, so the way in which to keep
cool, is to keep cool. Don't fret. "Fret
not thyself because of evil-doers," the good
book says, and they are golden words,
worthy of all acceptance, and to be repeated
daily in the synagogue. But "fret not
thyself at all" is a good saying. Quietly!
Quietly! Don't fret! The scribe attended
to his writing, and when he came down
among the others, where some of the older
folk were fuming very much as the babies
were, they said: "Why, you don't look
hot at all!" But, nevertheless, he was
undeniably warm.

Arm-chairs and rocking-chairs were carried out under the trees and pitched here
and there, wherever a tremor in the leaves

promised a breath of life-giving air. Around
the house the grass was green and fresh,
although in spots the ground had been worn
bare by passing feet, or left exposed because of the denser shade ; beyond, daisies
in myriads mottled the fields. Over the
porch a tulip tree carried its golden and
green cups high into the upper air. For a
moment the branches would rustle over
us, and a passing breeze would fan our
cheeks, then die away into utter stillness.

Scattered groups of two or three or more
appeared under the different trees, lads and
lasses here, feeling perhaps the glow of
warmth within equalling that without, or
perhaps merely skimming along the surface
in the irrepressible effervescence of youth ;
there pater and mater familias exchanging
the weekly Sunday greetings, with the restless young ones playing around in the grass,
or running out into the dusty road. The
scribe found an arm-chair shaded by a dense
maple and linden, and sank into it, armed
with a number of " Good Government,"
a volume of Thackeray's " Philip," and another of Molière. As in duty bound he
gave his attention first to the periodical,
and having done his duty in that direction,
fell back upon " Don Garcie." But as the

light breeze gently stirred the leaves, the
hot sun blinked through between them, and
the heavy air weighed upon the eyelids.
The book was closed, feet were thrust out,
and the head rested on the back of the
chair, while in the debatable land between
sleep and waking, thought floated aimlessly
among things present and absent, fact and
fancy.

Through eyes half-opened, a little toddling
figure in white is seen approaching, with
blue eyes and rosy cheeks and pouting lips.
"Won't you please get me some Marguer-
ites?" "Of course I will, my little one,"
and off we go hand in hand, among the
daisies. Again the border of dreamland is
reached, and then a red head ending in a
black nose is thrust into my hand, and the
owner thereof manifests a tendency to be
all over me at once. "Down, Rover, lie
down!" and with a push the affectionate
brute, for whose attentions I fear his master is not sufficiently grateful, is induced to
stretch himself out at my feet, breathing
heavily in the nervous fashion which the
distemper has bequeathed to him.

Passing along the village street toward
the post-office as the day is waning, the
reflection from the dry earth makes hot-

ter the hot air. Across the green of the
valley the distant hills and mountains rise
through the dusty haze, tier beyond tier,
clearly marked, like giant wave lines on a
mighty sea, disappearing gradually toward
the horizon. Behind the cloister, stretched
upon the fresh green grass under broad
spreading trees on westward sloping ground,
clad in white, lie maidens exchanging
maidenly confidences. The term is drawing to an end. The day of parting comes
on apace. For many, the school days are
ending, and closely knit friendships which
years have strengthened must now be sub-
jected to the test of separation, of new associations, of widening occupations, duties,
pleasures. The "curtain raiser" has been
played out; the curtain is about to fall;
then comes the prompter's bell, and it is
rung up again for the drama: what shall
this be? Ah! that for all there could be
something more of the rural simplicity, the
grateful repose of this favoured spot, than
our great cities with their feverish life
afford for many. May the heart burnings
be few, and while the recollections remain
always tender, may there not be intense
and bitter longing for that which cannot
return, for "the days that are no more."

Ah ! the heart sickness that must sometimes
come : —

> I have had playmates, I have had compan-
>   ions
> In my days of childhood, in my joyful school
>   days ;
> All, all are gone, the old familiar faces.
> —Some they have died, and some they have
>   left me,
> And some are taken from me ; all are de-
>   parted ;
> All, all are gone, the old familiar faces.

Bon voyage, Phillis and Phollis, one
going to meet the rising, one following the
setting sun. May the wild Atlantic quiet
her grim waves and bear the pilgrim safely
to the farther shore ! It is not for all of us
to tread historic paths ; to stand where the
brave deeds have been done which history
records, whatever brave deeds we may be
called upon to perform in the privacy of
our own lives ; not for us all to look upon
the monuments which attest past glory, to
see the noble remnants of olden art, the
quaint peculiarities of varying civilizations,
the finished culture of a riper world. May
the old world kindly receive the child of the
new, and may all the winds blow fair,
and safely guide the wanderer home again !

But let her beware of the lotos: —

— evermore
Most weary seem'd the sea, weary the oar,
Weary the wandering fields of barren foam.
Then some one said, " We will return no
    more ; "
And all at once they sang, " Our island home
Is far beyond the wave; we will no longer
    roam."

There is sweet music here that softer falls
Than petals from blown roses on the grass,
Or night dews on still waters between walls
Of shadowy granite, in a gleaming pass;
Music than gentlier on the spirit lies,
Than tir'd eyelids upon tir'd eyes:
Music that brings sweet sleep down from the
    blissful skies.

And in that newer world across the
prairies, which used to be the far West,
and has grown to be almost a part of the
East, whither the sun travels to shake off
upon the broad fields the drip of the sea,
may the welcome be a kindly one also, but
not so kindly as to cause Underledge to
fade away in the misty distance. There
be many paths among these green hills
yet untrod, many mysteries yet to be revealed.

JUNE 17, 1894.

XXVIII.

During the past week the frequent clink of the hammer has been heard upon the hill, and the walls have grown apace, heavy walls, with mighty stones in them, which make the inclosed space of the cottage look curiously small. But no hammer stroke has been heard on the face of the stones, and as they rise above the surface of the ground, the lichens and mosses give them an appearance of ancientness which is good to see. The masons have become interested in carrying out the enterprise as it was planned, and bid fair to produce a work with which they may quite properly be content.

The well has proved refractory, and it may yet need to be carried further into the bowels of the earth. But the fruit trees and most of the other plantings have taken kindly to their new home, and notwithstanding this second dry spell, with its intense heat, I must on the whole be satisfied with the appearance of the growing things. To-morrow or the next day, the favoured feathered bipeds, Leghorns and Plymouth Rocks, and Light Brahmas and Minorcas, should arrive from the city and take possession of the palatial quarters prepared for them, and if they do not incontinently take to laying at once, and lay with energy, they will be most ungrateful creatures. I am sure that any hen with the least æsthetic taste should feel proud to be so raised above the world, and provided with all the comforts of a luxurious home.

JUNE 17, 1894.

XXIX.

WE stand with bowed heads as the angel with the inverted torch passes swiftly by us. "The Lord gave, and the Lord hath taken away; blessed be the name of the Lord."

Let sorrow have her way. "The heart knoweth his own bitterness; and a stranger doth not intermeddle with his joy," neither with his sorrow. But it is permitted to others to shoulder in part the burdens of those that suffer most, and to go down into the dark valley with them. Do not try to smother the sorrow; it is the one right of the human being which none can question. We stand upon the brink and look out upon the vast unknown, and to our call no answer comes from the silence. Let us indulge the heartache, and commune with our own. The day was so fair; the bark kept on an even keel: —

Where lies the land to which the ship would
    go?
Far, far ahead, is all her seamen know.

We look again, and not a speck floats upon the surface of the waters. The call has gone forth, "and the spirit shall return unto God who gave it." We cannot quite realize it at first; we cannot understand it at all: wait a little; by and by we shall stand under it. The sad days of the past will grow dim in our memory; the dear, rich, happy days will come back once more to stay with us forever.

And as the years go by, and we gradually learn that there is only one thing for us to do, — to shower richer blessings around us, our own that would have been for him, and his, for whom we have become trustees, and whose trust we must fulfil to others, — then is the load adjusted, and we begin to understand.

And ever before us go the spirits that have left us, those

— we have loved long since, and lost awhile;

and when the long day wanes, and we feel aweary, the sounds of the present may attract us less, and in the future we may seem to see something of the past, and coupled with it that which we so much have longed for, — peace.

June 19, 1894.

XXX.

As I stand upon the hillside and look
across the green valley, where, notwithstanding another drought, the crops are making good headway ; when I remember that
whereas once great famines were a common
occurrence, now, thanks in good part to the
practice of forestalling, there is ever food
enough for all those that live upon the earth,
though here and there there are some who
fail to obtain it ; that, thanks to wonderful
labour-saving appliances, most articles of
necessity have been greatly reduced in cost,
and a vast number of things which were
once luxuries unattainable by any, are now
easily accessible by all but the very poor-
est ; that spite of " bad business " and
" hard times " there is enough and to spare
for all, while there are those always ready
to come to the assistance of the few whom
temporary conditions have thrown out of
their ordinary relation to the industries of
the community, — when I remember these
things, and that we are heirs of all the ages,

with the record of human experience lying
as an open page before us, and yet see the
wave of barbarism which is sweeping over
the earth, I feel weak.

The immediate prompting to this reflection is the dastardly assassination of Car-
not, which took place last night. In all
ages there have been assassinations of
rulers, and we have had previous instances
of the untimely taking off of those upon
whom in some measure depended the immediate progress of nations or of the race.
But here we have one of a constantly pro-
gressive series of incidents resulting from
deliberately organized barbarism. Society
in many countries is undermined in the
interest merely of destruction. This is
one, but perhaps not the most dangerous
aspect of the situation. Ideas and princi-
ples, as well as society and customs, are
undermined, and there is scarcely a truth
in business or social relations which history
and experience have taught, which is not
boldly repudiated and defied.

What is the cause of this, and what are
we to expect? It is difficult, I am not sure
that it is not impossible, to say. It all
seems so unnecessary, and yet we are apparently so impotent to prevent or cure it.

M

That the facts which I stated in opening are facts cannot be truthfully denied. The world is better off in material things than it ever was before. It has more opportunity for intellectual improvement than it ever had before. There is more chance for individual progress than there ever was before. Material development is more rapid than it ever was before. And yet all this seems to be accompanied by a condition of mental and moral collapse on the part of a considerable percentage of the human race.

If this condition only appeared in those who a hundred years ago would naturally have been classed as social nonentities, but who have now been brought forward as factors in nation and society, in an imperfect state of development, the problem would be an easier one. Unfortunately this does not seem to be the case. Examples appear in all ranks and among all classes, even the most favoured. Society's enemies are those of its own household, as well as those who have been forgotten. There seems to be a physical, mental, or moral fever running through the nations. May it prove but a transient epidemic, to be succeeded by a wholesome convalescence.

I cannot help thinking that it is not improbable that the disease is in some good
measure the result of the immensely rapid
development of discovery, invention, and
manufacture, of the stupendous changes of
the past century. These have been too
much for us. Animal and vegetable organ-
isms need time to fit them to new relations ;
we are out of key with our surroundings ;
we are in a state of ferment and unstable
equilibrium, of moral and mental flux.

We need to get away a little distance
from the crowd, to bare our foreheads to
the breeze and cool our throbbing temples.
Here we may lie among the daisies, and rest
ourselves until we can draw our breath in
steadiness and quite unconsciously. At
first the song of the lark or the bobolink
may hardly impress our ear. But after a
while we see the flashing of a wing, and
mayhap begin to realize a refreshing fragrance in the air. And probably it may
occur to us that there are such things as
false standards, and ignoble contests, and
wasted lives. What does the man or
woman need, after all ? Food and clothing
and shelter, a lift to the imagination, and
good companionship, — and how little they
cost ! A pest upon your gross ambitions !

Let us have again plain living and high thinking: the high thinking, at all events; for the plain living, fecund nature will hardly permit us that, unless we are determined to have it whether or no.

There is enough for us all and to spare, if we want only the very best things; and we know at least this much of the secret of the conversion of the world, — that each of us is the master of one life which can be turned to a good account.

I have been interested in the discussion caused by Mr. Godkin's suggestion that educated men distrust or regret universal suffrage. My observation leads me to believe that we are all, or most of us, more and more inclined to think forms of government of comparatively small account. All roads lead to Rome. Pretty nearly any form of government will work well in good hands; and without good citizens the best form which can be devised is valueless. We have said many proud things of our republicanism, and New York has trusted its fortunes to "the people." And what are we having revealed to us to-day? A closely knit combination of the sworn official conservators of the peace with the dregs of society, to prey upon and plunder the law-abiding members of the community.

Pah! Let us, at least for a while, get out where we can fill our lungs with God's own fresh air. And then let us put on the helmet and cuirass which may be appropriate, and with new strength in our arm, grasp the good sword Excalibur, or Nothung, if you please, and in knightly fashion throw ourselves into the thick of the fray, in defence of truth, justice, and purity.

JUNE 25, 1894.

XXXI.

As I cross the meadow and climb the hill in the morning to watch the growing walls, the tantalizing fog veiling and softening the heights but holding out little promise of rain, Mr. and Mrs. Robert of Lincoln give me their daily greeting. I fear that it is not all a manifestation of affection, but rather of alarm and solicitude for the brood hidden somewhere near by, among the tall grass. Mrs. Lincoln speaks prose in a pleasant chirping tone, but Robert has a very musical voice, and is lavish in its use. According to Wilson, he should now be changing his colour, and growing like unto his mate, but my friend is brilliant, a deep black on his breast and under side, and bright creamy yellow and white upon much of the upper part of his body and wings, much richer than my copy of Wilson represents him; while madam, on the contrary, is considerably duller than as represented, having a general brownish tone, tinged with yellow.

They circle around me, fluttering and soaring, and alight here and there upon the stalks of timothy, which bend but do not break under their weight, though from the size of the birds one would expect them to be much too heavy for the slender grass.

When I reach the upper part of the field I find the harvesters at work, the daisies, and such nutritious growth as they have permitted among them, going down crisply before the sharp scythes. I suppose that in time we may learn to see a like poetry in the action of the mowing machine with the driver riding atop; but as yet there is something which appeals to me much more strongly in the free swing and graceful swaying motion of the men as they follow one another step by step across the field, the grass falling in swaths at their side; while the musical ringing of the scythe stones upon the steel at intervals, I fear, is quite inimitable, and not to be compensated for by any substituted sound.

My poultry yard has received its consignment of fowls. They have been domesticated here for less than a week, and were at first disposed to be very timid and flighty. But already they have become accustomed to Nicholas John and myself, and this morning the handsome Minorca rooster came and took grain from my hand, with many encouraging expressions to the members of his harem. His interest in their welfare, however, did not prevent him from devouring what was before him as rapidly as he could, and disposing of it all, just before the ladies became ready to show the same confidence in my good intentions.

My Brown Leghorn cock appears very much discouraged. Since Sunday morning he has been dull and moping, supporting himself about as much upon his head as his heels; and wild as he was before, he is not now disposed to take more than a step or two when I put my hands upon him, and only eats and drinks when assisted. I fear that his belligerent propensities have led him to try conclusions with the huge Plymouth Rock rooster in the next yard, and that he has come to grief in the meshes of the woven wire fence between them.

I suppose that you do not realize that I am merely beating about the bush. To-day the term ends, and the cloisters are closed. The dear old lumbering stage-coach with its various tenders have made

their several trips, laden inside and out
with hopes and fears, sorrows and joyful
anticipations, as well as with human bodies.
Hands and kerchiefs have been waved, and
kisses thrown, and the teary eyes tried
bravely to seem as though there were no
showers within hail. But ah! there is no
drought that long affects the fount which so
readily flows at the tap of the affections.

Go up, thou bald-head! Has life so
worn with thee that all thy papillæ have
become seared and callous, no longer re-
sponding to the touch of thy fellows?
Has all sentiment come to seem mere sen-
timentality, and naught real and true except bonds and stocks, and quotations in
the market, fine carriages and fast horses,
dollars and cents? If so, I pity thee.
Good by, bathos and spectacle, — a good
riddance to you. Do not try to pump feeling from wells drilled in the social hardpan. But if there be anything truer,
richer, more lasting, and more worthy than
the strong attachments of human beings, I
know not what it is. If we may not testify
to the tie which binds heart to heart, until
the eyelids are closed, and the cool pit is
opened, and the dull clods fall upon the
straw, then let us, like the stricken deer,

quietly creep away, and lie down for the last time in the solitude of the remote forest, for life has no more for us within its gift.

My brothers in arms, have we not summered and wintered together, have we not had a common playtime, and have we not fought side by side in social and political frays, as with beasts at Ephesus? Have we not tested each other's temper, and found what manner of men we are? Do we not know that so long as life holds out we shall be ready to rally at the call, and present a bold front to the ills that threaten any one of us, or the commonweal? Then go to! Let us join hands, and look into each other's eyes, and frankly confess that we are kindred spirits, and in our feeling a little more than kin and not less than kind.

And now the footfall is silent on the doorstep. Away in the distance, the rumbling coach takes its course over the valley, and the dust has fallen upon the track which it made. Close the windows and draw the curtains, and permit the spiders to weave their webs across the sashes.

Let us go up upon the mountain, and look for the locusts.

JUNE 26, 1894.

XXXII.

I THINK that it is nearly four weeks since we have had a shower sufficiently heavy to soak through the dust on the roads, and the ground is parched as though it had been baked in an oven. And yet the forests and the meadows remain green, and even where the hay has been harvested, the grass does not seem burned to a crisp. Day after day we watch the storm-clouds forming around us; we hear the muttering of distant thunder, and, as night approaches, see the electric signals flash from cloud to cloud; it is thunder to right of us, thunder to left of us, thunder in front of us; occasionally a cool breeze from another valley comes to inform us of the grateful showers that have fallen there. The ladies tell me that the air is laden with moisture, and that consequently dainty dresses, quietly hanging in the closet, contract their skirts by inches, as if to escape contact with a wet earth; nevertheless, the would-be welcome rain tarries yet in the offing.

I have a new Brown Leghorn rooster,
master of the clan *vice* the first incumbent,
incapacitated, and since transferred to another sphere. And he is a true squire of
dames, brilliant in his plumage, imposing
in his carriage, and withal courtly and
generous in his manners. In the latter
respect, I confess that he greatly surprised
me, after my experience with his cousin
from Minorca. He quickly ventured to
take grain from my hand, or from the
ground close beside me, but instead of immediately swallowing it, would hold it in
his beak, clucking an encouraging invitation to the ladies of his family, and, as if
realizing that their enterprise might not
be sufficient to bring them quite so close
to the great ogre, man, would move off
two or three steps, and lay the grain upon
the ground, continuing his cheering calls.
Often he has to pick up and lay down the
same grain two or three times, before he
finds a customer for it, but at length it will
be called for, and he will look on most
benignly while it is being disposed of.
Sometimes it is necessary for him to go
through the process of laying down the
grain, and scratching about it, before his
coy consorts can be encouraged to approach.

Occasionally he swallows a grain, just to keep up his strength for the work in hand ; but I do not think that he takes more than one out of a dozen, which is much less than his share.

But he has the defects of his virtues, and is a good deal of a swash-buckler. He is of the time of Louis XIII. and XIV., and reminds me now of the dainty Aramis, and now of Athos, Porthos, and the rough and ready D'Artagnan. He will vary his amusements by periodically facing his neighbour, the Plymouth Rock rooster in the adjoining yard, like his lamented predecessor ; and this morning he managed to get over the high fence, and to give the latter such a drubbing that he was fain to retire into the privacy of his own apartments, with both eyes closed, and generally such a wreck as was pitiful to behold. I hope that this interview has so far settled their differences that hereafter peace may reign upon the confines of their dominions.

Strangely enough, the locusts have not invaded the precincts of the village. Two or three days ago, I saw one fluttering through my dining-room that is to be, but it was the only one that I have seen this side of the hills. In the hottest part of

the day we still hear the distant buzzing of
their calls; but it is not near so loud as it
was ten days ago, and it does not attract
our attention in the early morning as it did
then. Wings are found here and there
upon the street, the related bodies having,
I imagine, been disposed of by the birds.

A week ago, I went up on the hills to
make a nearer acquaintance with the company. When fairly among them, the air
rang with their note, as if with the whirring of a considerable collection of light
machinery and gearing, with now and then
a curious rising inflection. It is quite
unlike the hot, dry rattle of our ordinary
locusts. I saw many of the insects themselves, but they were far from being as
numerous as I remember them in the
Pennsylvania brood of a certain year that
shall be nameless. May I not have my
reticences? If there was a pre-diluvian
period which I can look back upon, let us
assume it to have been vaguely a Saturnian
era, a Golden age, without beginning and
without end, the glamour of which still
lingers upon the hills of to-day.

On this recent excursion, I did not see
any of the insects emerging from their
shells, as I frequently did in those early

days; but I saw many of these shells, sometimes two or three of them left upon a single leaf, having the opening in the back through which the insect escaped. And many of the locusts were busily at work boring the holes in which to deposit their eggs. This they do most industriously, and it is far from being an easy task. I watched one for perhaps nearly ten minutes, effecting a single perforation; and sometimes these appear at intervals of a half inch or so, for a distance of as much as a foot, or a foot and a half, along a single branch, apparently, though I cannot say certainly, made by a single female.

The ovipositor is a horny, sting-like appendage attached near the middle of the lower side of the body. It is about a third of an inch long and slightly curved backward, and the perforation is effected by gripping the branch or twig tightly with the feet, and contracting the legs so as to force the instrument diagonally through the bark into the wood. The muscular exertion required must be very great, and the ovipositor is nearly withdrawn and again thrust into the wood over and over before the work is completed.

I suppose that it is well known that little

or no serious damage is done by the insects through eating in this stage of existence. The devastation produced in the woods and among the scattered trees is caused by the destruction of innumerable twigs and small branches by the boring for the deposit of eggs, this resulting shortly in the death of these twigs. I think it is not improbable that some active poison is inserted at the time the egg is laid. At all events, in most cases the twig quickly dies and becomes brittle, and is broken off by the wind, and then falling to the ground, the new generation is permitted, as soon as released from the egg, to sink below the surface and begin the period of seventeen years of subterranean existence, from which these which I have been observing have just emerged.

JULY 2, 1894.

XXXIII.

How beautiful is the rain !
After the dust and heat,
In the broad and fiery street,
In the narrow lane,
How beautiful is the rain !

THE leaden clouds gather around us and shut off the hot rays of the sun, and the thunder comes nearer than we have had it in many weeks. But we have become incredulous, and I hear the patter of the falling drops upon the leaves over my head before I realize that there is any need for me to gather up my books and papers, and seek shelter under the neighbouring roof. For a moment the drops fall merrily, and bury themselves in the finely powdered dust upon the drive outside the window; but before the surface has been moistened all over, the supply is cut off, a break appears in the curtain which covers the heavens, and the sun gleams through again as though like the clown at the circus, to say, " Here we are again ! "

N

But never mind ; there are three or four little puddles upon the floor of the porch, large enough to reflect the branches waving in the freshened breeze, a grumble is heard now from one quarter and now from another where heavy clouds cover most of the sky, and " we may be happy yet."

Yesterday, when I parted from Blondin after our cosy lunch in one of those quiet little foreign places which you will find here and there in old dwelling-houses upon the cross streets in the metropolis, and took my way to spend an hour at the club before train time, the sunshine came almost as hot from the blistering pavement of the dusty and noisy street as from the heavens above. But on an inner balcony at the club-house, which I had quite to myself at this hour, it was gratefully cool and quiet. My hour passed all too quickly, and I soon found myself amid the throng at the neighbouring station. The bull reigns in the zodiac, and the air is heavy and the pulse high as the holiday crowds, flushed and flurried, gather in the long trains to flee away from the city for a breath of fresh country air. It is not until the Bronx comes in sight, with the appropriate accent of a *blanchisseuse* upon the bank, with clean white garments

scattered upon the grass around her, that
the weight lifts a little, and we realize once
more that life is worth living. Even here
much is sordid and mean, and it is but a
touch now and then which lets us out into
the infinite. "Hop" Smith, the versatile,
tells me that "A Day at Laguerre's" was
drawn with absolute truth, and I am sure
that he believes it. But then he is of the
fortunate ones who evolve their own facts
from the nature of their constitution, and
carry with them an atmosphere which
causes the light to touch with a tender glow
the most common things. And who would
not rather see Mambrino's helmet than a
barber's basin, and find an inspiration to
knightly deeds in the Dulcinea del Toboso?
If I may not think my geese all swans, let
me never keep a flock to squawk at my
coming.

But the French at Laguerre's are retiring
before Guiseppe and Pietro and Giacomo,
and the peasants of sunny Italy are, tempo-
rarily at least, taking the place of the vola-
tile and genial Gaul; and they have brought
their barbarisms with them. They are not
our barbarisms, of the counting-house and
the shop and the mine, but the hot blood of
the South, the quick word, and the knife.

Whether is better the mean tawdry life of vulgar commonplace, high or low, gilded or unvarnished, or the life that rests on a word, a flash, a blow, — good-night ! — Say rather, which is worse ?

At least this is to be said, — while there is life there is hope, and it takes so small an aperture for the soul to creep through ! "'Tis not so deep as a well, nor so wide as a church door; but 'tis enough, 'twill serve." Our vulgarisms are the meanest of the mean, and we have enough of them, Heaven knows. But if "There is some soul of goodness in things evil," as Shakespeare says, we have a right to hope that in the coming days there may be ever more of the sweet and wholesome growing therefrom, as the richest flowers spring from the soil where we have buried most of that which was noisome and vile.

While I have been writing, we have had another shower, and again the sunlight lies upon the freshened fields. The contribution has not been large, but perhaps the charm of the evil eye has been broken, and better days are in store for us.

JULY 4, 1894.

XXXIV.

It is said that every man should be the architect of his own fortunes, and I think that each should be, at least in a degree, the architect of his own house. It is not a bad plan for him to be to some extent its builder also. It should represent his ideas, if he has any, in its arrangement and construction; he should watch it grow under his eyes, look after the setting of the roots, follow it up into the air, place a loving hand on its stones and timbers, know intimately what is contained in its walls and partitions as well as what is contained between them, and do something himself toward putting them together.

I know that it is said that a shoemaker should stick to his last, and that when a man is his own lawyer, he has a fool for a client. And there is much truth in both of these statements. The professional is, or should be, indispensable; but he cannot replace the client in his knowledge of the thing which is most appropriate to him.

One would not wish to have some one else select all his books and pictures for him, or even his wife and children.

I have followed with a critical and caressing eye the growth of the cottage on the hillside, and have experienced a glow of satisfaction in seeing the manner in which the irregular blocks found their places, and I hope the lichens will take kindly to the new angle at which the sun and wind must reach them. When the cellar was covered I went down into the cool shadow, and felt myself in a manner at home, though the outlook was somewhat as through the port-holes of a ship, excepting that the deep blue sea was replaced by the green valley and the deep blue hills on the horizon. And I walked the rough floor, as a captain might walk his quarter-deck, and looked through the door-frames, and the irregular apertures where the window-frames ought to be, and began to realize more fully that all this vast outdoors is mine, whatever futile efforts my thousand neighbours may make to retain their proprietorship.

To-day I went up on the side of the ledge and selected certain special stones which I desired to have worked into the walls. And some of them I brought down myself upon a rickety wheelbarrow. How astonishingly a wheelbarrow wobbles when you have a somewhat heavier load on board than you are quite equal to! It really is the tipsiest sort of a conveyance, and you feel yourself a kindred spirit. But I succeeded in completing the journey with all but the heaviest, and for the raising and transfer of this I was compelled to call for assistance. And then came the placing, in which I became a free and accepted mason, pushing with my little might to swing the boom of the derrick into place, and handling the crowbar in the adjustment upon the corner. It is true that I had the assistance of the professionals, or rather, assisted them, which being interpreted means that they probably wished me in Ballyhack, wherever that may be. However, they were very amiable, and let me have my way, and I am sure that the house will be a better house — for me — because I have had a hand in its construction.

The trap-rock of which I am building will stand any amount of pressure when well placed, but it is very brittle when struck, and sometimes breaks anywhere but where one desires, and flies into a dozen pieces. Therefore we have, so far as possible, to secure such masses as will

serve us without alteration, and it being
understood that the best face is to be
shown to the world, this costs a good deal
of time. But the game is amply worth the
candle. I verily believe that no such beautiful wall, considering its location and purpose, could be erected of any other material. The softer mosses, I suppose, will
all disappear under the greater exposure,
and perhaps some of the larger and coarser
lichens also; but the finer and more delicate
ones, I am sure, will remain and continue to
grow. And the weather stains are also certainly permanent. When the cement in
the cracks is thoroughly dried, it is covered
with a whitish efflorescence, which is very
effective, though perhaps it has rather too
much accent. It will doubtless, however,
gradually tone down under the action of
the dust, little of this though there be,
which can wander hitherward across the
fields; certainly none that can be perceived
in the air. The vines, I am sure, will take
kindly to this rough surface, and I shall
only hesitate to let them cover too much
of it.

JULY 9, 1894.

XXXV.

LOST !

CAN you imagine anything that could cause a more hopeless sinking of your heart than to have it suddenly announced to you in the gloaming that your child had strayed away and was lost? The light lingers on the edge of the sky above the hills, the steel gray showing that the dust has recently been washed out of it. The stars be-gem the vault overhead, and the crescent moon has just begun to throw down a faint reflected light, a suggestion only of what she may do when she grows older and stronger. There is an uncertain mingling of the daylight, which is fast fading, and the lamplight, which hardly serves to do more than to make the coming darkness visible, and the dew is falling, and there is a suspicion of a chill in the air, — and the child is lost.

Quick! The darkness grows apace. Whither shall we go? Down behind the inn to the brook, or by the road to the river? Or may it possibly be along the village street that he strayed? Or — you remember Charley Ross?

Hurry! He has not been seen for half an hour, — an hour. Look — everywhere! Bring the horse and the buckboard. Let us fly!

Well, well! It was a false alarm. The little fellow had strayed away some hundreds of yards, and had been hospitably entreated by a thoughtless neighbour; and here he is by his mother's side again, and all is well. And the full eyes of the mother say, Good friends, pardon me. I am very sorry to have alarmed you so, but — but — he was lost! My child was lost!

JULY 9, 1894.

XXXVI.

I suppose it was fated that Pandora should lift the cover from the box. We may wish that she had sat upon it, or tumbled it into the sea, or disposed of it in some other way, but it is of no use. The box was to be opened. That way lay the path of the race, and take any by-road you might, you were sure to come out upon the same track at last.

But I think that the Greeks only had a forecast of what might be, and that the box was not really opened until very recently. The ancients thought that they had puzzling questions to deal with, but they were mistaken. They might badger their brains about "Fixed fate, free will, foreknowledge absolute"; but these, being insoluble riddles which they might take or leave, were simply personal problems, as were most others with which they had to deal. It was left to the age of the printing press, steam, and electricity, above all to the age of the "walking delegate," to propound puzzles which must be dealt with if human society is to continue to exist, but with which we are apparently powerless to deal.

Up on the slope at Underledge the ground is not now as moist as we should like it to be, though the weather is absolutely perfect. Some of us are very poor, and none of us feel very rich; but we get something to eat almost every day, and if we do not have a good thick juicy beefsteak at each meal, we remember having read of persons who had made a fair repast upon shoe leather. We look about us, and we see labouring men of moderate calibre, who have never had more than a labouring man's modest wages, who have married and brought up families, and who, withal, have established and own comfortable homes in which they live under their own vines and cherry trees. They get their dollar and a half a day when they can earn it, and when they cannot earn it they dig in the garden, or tend the baby, and hope for the time when they can.

Most of us receive a daily newspaper, or if we do not take one ourselves, we borrow our neighbour's, or we hear what the paper contains when we go down to the post-office. And nowadays the paper contains the most remarkable tales. It appears that millions of dollars worth of property has been burned or otherwise destroyed; that many more millions worth of damage has been effected by the derangement of business; that numbers of lives have been sacrificed, and incalculable misery has been inflicted over a vast extent of territory by combinations of men banded together to prevent other men, if possible, from doing just what our labouring men have done at Underledge, just what the intelligent and industrious workingman has been doing for several thousand years past, —the best that he could do for himself and his family, as an honest, self-respecting member of society.

This is the situation as it appears to us. We suppose that a man can give up working if he chooses, if he thereby breaks no contract, and does not compel others to support him in idleness; but there, so far as we can perceive, his right ends. When he undertakes to prevent others from working who desire to do so, he is acting as an enemy of the first principle upon which civilization and society rest; he is guilty of treason against the race, and there is no punishment which the race can impose which is a fit measure of his guilt. This treason must be put down if it takes every able-bodied man, and the cripples also, and every dollar's worth of property in existence ; it must be put down at the cost of everything which society possesses ; at the cost, if need be, of wiping off the face of the land all that has been put upon it during the past four hundred years, leaving a clean page, upon which, let us hope, to write a more cheerful history.

This is the way it looks to us at Underledge, and we are ready to do our part, if called upon, to correct the abuse. But it seems to us a not unimportant fact in connection with this time and the future, that there are said to be hundreds of thousands of persons throughout the country, scattered here and there all over the land, who are associated in this movement, or who sympathize with it, or who, under slightly different conditions, would take similar action, and that it is impossible to show them the utter folly of their beliefs, and of their course ; that governors of states, United States senators and representatives, and lesser officials innumerable, give aid and comfort to them ; that ministers of the gospel and college professors pander to their fallacious fancies and stimulate their wild hopes, and thus promote their destructive work. Not that all these counsel or countenance the illegal and violent acts referred to, but that that which they advocate or approve or suggest will lead to such results, just as surely as night follows the day. And all the while we remember that this is a "popular" government, and that in these times a popular government usually means in practice not a competition for the suffrages and support of the intelligent and thoughtful, but bids by the machinists of both the leading parties, and often of the outlying factions, for the votes of all the crack-brained, the turbulent, the dissatisfied, and the lazy.

So we do not look upon the field of the immediate future, either here or abroad, as a bed of roses. It seems much more likely to be the paradise of the demagogue and the visionary, and the inferno of the quiet citizen who wishes to "live in the spirit."

Nevertheless, we desire to keep our heads level. We remember that somebody wrote recently "Don't fret," and we intend to remember the charge. We recall that during the July riots in New York, in 1863, there came a heavy shower, and the mob scattered like sheep. And we hope for some cooling baptism that will send people back to their homes where they can collect their thoughts, and perhaps recall, or have a revelation of the fact, that salvation does not come to masses, but to individuals. We are an inventive people, and we have machines performing a great variety of operations; but, so far as we have heard, none has yet been received at the patent office warranted to make the world over again as good as new, but upon a different plan; and we would suggest to the various philosophers who are busily employed in devising such machines that an honest day's work can be much more easily and effectively performed by strengthening, polishing, and lubricating the machinery already in use, and by doing themselves, and inducing others to do, a little more faithful labour than has been hitherto accomplished. These are homely remedies, but wholesome, like the cooling herbs of our grandmothers, more reliable than any patent medicines, and likely to prove more efficient than the drugs of Debs, Bellamy, Most, *et id genus omne.*

JULY 10, 1894.

XXXVII.

LAST night the heavens came down in grateful showers. They were not all that we desired, but they were more than we had had before in many weeks, and we recognize the bounty. And so I am sure do tree and vine and herb, if there is any virtue in the expressions with which they have greeted the morning. The wilted leaves have become again firm and green, the branches and twigs graceful and elastic, the blossoms bright and clear.

Upon the unwritten domestic calendar the memorandum appears, "About this time look out for young chickens," and therefore my first visit on my return was to the poultry-yard. And I hope that I was duly thankful when I found one little elliptical fluffy duffer as the net result of two good "clutches" of eggs. And I hope that he or she — or "he-sh," should I say? — feels in a proper degree the responsibility thrown upon "himr" as the sole representative of so many promising beginnings.

o

Already within the brief period of my absence the infant had pecked a way into the world through the crisp limestone wall by which he had been surrounded, and had begun to push "hisr" pin-feathers. Its voice was at least twice as big as its body, and attested as good a pair of lungs as one could wish. Yet a little while, and doubtless the infant prodigy will bridle and strut with all the dignity appropriate to the first-born on the new estate.

The house has made good progress, and the masons are completing their work. Four walls with many and large port-holes form the hull of the vessel, and we shall soon be ready for the top-hamper.

The persistency with which most of the inhabitants of the garden continued to grow during the drought was a constant marvel. Doubtless last night's rain will help them greatly, although the ground is not soaked for a depth of more than from one to four inches, in reverse degree according to its firmness. But even before this came, the general appearance was good, and some things were doing finely. My sweet peas, my "sweet sixteen," the sole representatives in the garden of those that neither toil nor spin, gave me a great jar full of blos-

soms yesterday morning, and there were
more in the afternoon, and again to-day.
And how lovely they are! People almost
seemed to have forgotten them until ten
years ago; they were flowers of the "old
gardens." And then Dame Fashion took
them up, — by a strange inadvertence making a happy choice, — and strangely enough
she has not yet discarded them. They were
too lovely for her favour to spoil them; but I
am not sure that those of us who love flowers
for what they are, will not find them sweeter
and dearer when she shall have passed
them by.

The season is waxing older. The fragrant
odour of the milkweeds here and there fills
the air, the wild carrot lifts its jewelled lace
over the recently mown fields; two days
ago I saw the golden-rod by the roadside in
the old Bay State, and the dark red clusters
of the chokecherry bedeck the hedgerows.
The days grow perceptibly shorter, ere yet
the year has reached its climax.

Familiar faces are missing at the inn,
and familiar voices are silent. Already
their owners are doubtless far, far away,
speeding over the summer seas, perhaps — I
hope surely — to find balm in the Gilead of
another clime and other scenes, among an

alien people. We shall miss them sorely, but what would you? "As ships that pass in the night." Yea, verily. Through the years it is "Hail!" and "Farewell!" But is it not a pleasant thought that here and there, scattered over the wide, wide world, there are those whom you may never again meet, but with whom you have memories in common, those into whose eyes and hearts you have sometime looked far enough to see truth therein, and to know that there is an unbound freemasonry in which you and they are forever comrades for weal or for woe? What matters it though seas roll their waves between, though ripening years sink away into the eternal silence? "Age cannot wither" the unchanging past.

And so, as through the night watches the stanch vessels pass, and fade away in the darkness, we breathe a loving benison upon the disappearing craft, and bid them godspeed. It may be that the storm clouds lower, the lightning flashes, the thunder reverberates from mass to mass, the surging waves plunge angrily before the driving gale. But above it all, the stars are shining silently in the infinite spaces, and beyond the tempest, and sometimes even in the heart of it, there is peace.

JULY 22, 1894.

XXXVIII.

In times of drought such as this, the fountains of nature seem to get into the condition of a pump which has ceased to "draw," at which you may work and work to heart's content, or discomfort, but nothing comes. *Parturiunt montes, nascitur ridiculus mus.* Yesterday the mercury in the thermometer mounted higher and higher during the day, like the price of gold upon the famous Good Friday, until it hovered on the edge of ninety-eight degrees, and the aerial currents marked an even temperature with the vital ones. Then came the gathering of a tempest; thin clouds formed over the sky, becoming from moment to moment more dense; heavy and threatening cumulus masses arose in the south, and gradually covered the heavens, south, east, and west; magnificent thunder-heads climbed toward the zenith; a deep leaden-blue veil spread over all that portion of the vault, occasionally rent by sharp flashes of lightning, followed by reverberating thunder, and in a brief time the whole sky was shrouded; we took our places on the front porch to inhale the freshening breeze and watch the oncoming of the anticipated torrents, somewhat awed, as most are, by the outburst of heaven's artillery; but not one solitary moistening drop did the storm vouchsafe us. The clouds gradually thinned and parted in the west; with the coming night the stars again looked out upon the lower world, and the torrid earth radiated its burning heat into the night air.

This morning the sun again stares down upon the parched fields, and the mercury again climbs slowly and steadily toward the centennial mark. While walking along the dusty road, and crossing the open fields, the heat seemed almost to burn into the brain and cause it to sizzle. The long sharp rattle of the common locust marks the day with its characteristic note. But here, sitting upon the bank at the border and in the shade of my wood which masks the low cliff, a pleasant breeze soothes my bare brow and revives the spirit of life within me.

I wonder whether I can picture the scene? Behind me the wind awakens a soothing murmur among the trees, through which the hot sunlight filters here and there, flickering pleasantly upon the moving leaves. Before me fall away the gently undulating slopes of the "mountain meadow," with the poultry-yard between me and the highway, close to the edge of the wood, from which from time to time I hear the cackle of the hens or the crowing of the cocks, some of which, with characteristic curiosity, stray down to the corner nearest to me and watch me at my writing. Were I nearer, I should also hear the pleasant chirping of the downy chicks, now numbering a dozen or more, clustered confidingly around their careful foster-mother. The line of shadow from the woods extends a short distance in front of me; then comes the open sunny field, from which the hay was recently harvested, now speckled over with the branching stems and flat white crowns of the wild carrot; beyond and slightly to the left, the slender village spire lifts itself against the distant hills, overtopping a curtain of deep green trees. It was of this that Elihu Burritt, "the learned blacksmith," said, that as he, then a little urchin, looked down upon it from Sunset Rock, he felt as one should do in looking for the first time upon St. Peter's, and thought that if the big rooster (which in those days was really a crown) should crow, "the rude forefathers of the hamlet" up in heaven would certainly recognize his voice, and know that he was an Underledge rooster, and that he brought news of the faithfulness of their successors.

Upon the slope directly in front of me, and fifty or sixty yards away, are the drying walls of the cottage, with their wide-open eyes, and heaped around is the lumber for the superstructure, which during the next sennight will so greatly change the appearance of the building. The rapid fall of the ground beyond conceals from my view, from this point, the picturesque pasture and the damp, green marsh; but I see the orchard beyond, then here and there a chimney or bit of roof rising among the trees at the north end of the village, then the line of great elms and maples indicating the course of the river. The farm lands of the intervale show varying shades of green and brown, spotted here and there with scattered trees, and divided by a few fences scarcely visible from here, and wild hedgerows, with a considerable farmstead in the middle distance, two or three isolated houses and barns, an occasional cluster of bits of roof indicating a village, with now and then a faint church spire. On a moderate hill nearly to the north, and eight or ten miles away, I see distinctly in the noon-day light the long walls of the great new house of a New York merchant. To the east of north, and on my right, runs out the line of high hills which abut upon the "second mountain" and form the rim of our basin to the east, with gently sloping cultivated fields between, and still show-ing on the hither side a remnant of the old " Pilgrims' Path " of the colonial time. Due north, and fifteen miles away, rise from the valley the two singular hills which form its portal.

Nearly the whole country seems covered with forest, though most of it is young or of moderate age,— probably none " prime-val," as I have heretofore said,— and here and there in the distance I see a space marked by recent severe cutting, or browned by a late forest-fire. Beyond the valley the hills lie in ranges, almost seeming, toward "Satan's kingdom " in the northwest. or thirty miles away in the far north, to float in the hot and hazy air ; and they recede until they become indistinguishable in tint from the sky which falls to meet them.

Over all this spreads the sky, fading from

a translucent blue overhead to a warm pale
tint above the hills, with detached fleecy
clouds which seem as if every drop of
moisture had been squeezed out of them,
and they were of no more promise to the
vegetable or animal world than so much
gun-cotton; while marshalled around the
horizon are the faint blue-pink heaps
which from hour to hour hold out to us
the promise which they never keep.

This is the scene upon which I look.
And as I write I hear the characteristic
note of the thistle bird as it plunges along
in its diving flight; in front, flutters a yellow butterfly, and above soar two or three
swallows seeking for insects; the line of
shadow draws nearer to my feet, and I
notice the leaves of the melon vines wilting
in the fervent heat. And still the trees
wave and bend before the breeze, and I
seem to hear a low rumble as of distant
thunder. Hush! Hark! Yes, it surely is;
but still the eye sinks far away into the
blue of the sky, and the hot sunlight beats
upon the hillside.

JULY 29, 1894.

XXXIX.

O Tannenbaum, O Tannenbaum,
Wie treu sind deine Blätter.
Du grünst nicht nur zur Sommerzeit,
Nein, auch im Winter wenn es schneit.
O Tannenbaum, O Tannenbaum,
Wie treu sind deine Blätter.

YESTERDAY morning we went up into a neighbouring wood to select some cedar trees whose trunks shall serve as pillars for the porches. They are to be straight and firm, and are to have the branches cut off and to have the bark stripped from them, but otherwise they are to be left in their natural condition. Branches of the same, not too pronounced in their eccentricity, will be used for the balustrade and the trellis beneath. Then honeysuckles and other vines will be invited to lend their graceful tracery in decoration, and their grateful shade from the southern, eastern, and western sun.

It is almost a pity that the living trees cannot be taken and made to serve our

turn. They come into our lives in many
ways, and at all times and seasons. How
beautiful they were last winter, laden down
with the fleecy shower, the dark green of
their leaves contrasting with the whiteness
of their burden of snow! And at the
Christmastide some of their race bore a
wondrous variety of fruit, of which the
gem of all was the kindly feeling which inspired the festival. And now as the warm
sun upon their branches brings out the
spicy odours, we recognize the very essence
of the forest in its completeness. Below
us, winding about among the roots in the
bottom of the little valley, tumble and
gurgle the waters of the " Great brook," with
trout doubtless lurking here and there, seeking shelter from the heat under the shadow-
ing banks of the deeper pools ; while on the
other side, above the slope, tall hemlock
trees spread their protecting branches until
they interlace, leaving open spaces below
quite clear of underbrush, carpeted with
brown leaves, and forming solemn, shadowy
aisles.

I hardly think that the first and strongest impression that we get of the German
people as we see them in this country, is
the poetic. And yet how full they are of

music, and how their songs and their literature are permeated by the impressions
derived from nature, and how strong a love
for it they manifest ! Some of us prefer to
take these things diluted with a smaller
amount of beer, and prefer the scent of
roses alone, rather than mixed with those
of tobacco and other things. But even these
are more like the odour of sanctity than some
things which are characteristic of our urban
life.

On a festival, the German instinctively
seeks the country and the woodlands.
The Schwarzwald and the Böhmerwald,
and the Thüringerwald maintain their
hold upon him, whether he comes from
their shadowy recesses or not. And it is
fair to believe that his homely wholesome
family life has some not unnatural connection with this life in the open air, and
among our brothers who draw their sustenance directly from the soil.

The proper study of mankind is man.
Yes, doubtless. And the first claimant on
our aid and bounty, if we have them to
give, is likewise man. But there are many
ways in which this study can be made
and this aid extended, and it is not unfair
to assume that something can be gained

even yet by "going back to nature." And by this I do not mean throwing away what has been earned in the past, and making shipwreck of civilization, but rather the attempt to assimilate this new food if we have not yet become quite used to it, by taking it in instalments, as we might test a boletus or a coprinus atramentarius, falling back for our mainstay upon good wholesome brownbread, potatoes, and roast beef, which by long experience we have proved to be reliable diet. But there, I am not a Paganini, and I think that I have played upon that one string more than once before. It is a good string, however, and susceptible of infinite variations of tone, and I am not sure that a master could not play upon it all the music with which life is full.

JULY 29, 1894.

XL.

I SUPPOSE that most people, at some time or other in their careers, " get their come-upance," to use the vernacular of these New England States. This was my reflec-tion, as I went up from the inn yesterday and turned into High street, when I beheld upon the descending road an army of dark-hued men from the shores of the Medi-terranean, not with banners, but with pick-axes and shovels, with great wires and cross-ties and iron rails, digging and pulling and hammering, drawing and quartering, —and realized that vengeance was being meted out to the Goths and the Vandals, the Ostrogoths and the Visigoths, for their descent upon the sunny South a millennium ago. And taking refuge from Scylla, I came near unto falling into Charybdis; for there in front of me, turning into the street at the other end, was a wandering troubadour, pre-sumably of the same stock, with an instru-ment of torture like unto an upright piano loaded upon a go-cart. I incontinently fled

into the fields, hearing behind me, but subdued in the distance, the mocking tintinnab-
ulation of the fiend-like machine.

The trolley is knocking at our doors ; the
uncouth poles already mar the prospect, and
we hear the sharp ring of iron upon iron as
the spikes are driven home. It is no longer
a question of possibilities ; the emergency
is upon us, and there is little room left for
speculation as to what changes may be im-
pending. With characteristic subjection of
common rights and convenience to individual ease and advantage, our main highway
— outside of the village — which at places is
but narrow, is sacrificed to the intruder, and
wicked pedestrians, and riders upon horseback, and drivers in carriages, must take
their chances of disastrous accident or
"electrocution."

So far, thanks to close supervision, no
serious damage has been done to our finest
trees, and we hope to save these from
destruction. If we succeed in this, we shall
be more fortunate than many; but we view
the possibility of an attack upon our Main
street with a shudder of apprehension. If
the cars were not so very heavy, we should
be disposed to say that they should only
pass that way, if at all, over our own

bodies. Halting a little short of this degree of self-devotion, we at least solemnly
vow that this outrage shall be endured
only when all legal preventives shall have
failed.

What a farce it is to call a country "civilized," in which such questions are liable
from day to day to be presented, to chal-
lenge the firmness and public spirit, and to
consume the time and strength of the intelligent citizen! Such a proposition should
answer itself as promptly and conclusively as
a similar proposition is answered in the old
nursery rhyme : —

> Said Aaron to Moses,
> ' Let's cut off our noses.'
> Said Moses to Aaron,
> ' It's the fashion to wear 'em.'

I hope that we are gradually learning, — at
least some of us, — " that a man's life con-
sisteth not in the abundance of the things
which he possesseth," nor in the viands
which appear upon his table, nor in the
garments that he wears, though all these
things may in subordination contribute to it ;
and that the glory and merit of a village
no more consist in the number of its inhabitants irrespective of their kind, in the

P

bustle upon its streets, nor in the gaudiness of its decorations.

I think that one of the most singular exhibitions of folly that we have ever seen was the struggle which followed the late census, the emulation between different localities, each seeking to establish its superiority by enumerating the bodies, not the souls, of its inhabitants. As if a hundred underfed, undereducated, undeveloped, and unhappy families were worth one homely, quiet household, full of the joy of life and love and helpfulness! As if the ideal toward which the world is struggling were a nest of squirming maggots!

It seems to me that there has been a little chastening of this spirit within these later years, and that quality is gradually attaining something of its rightful recognition as compared with quantity. And we, as we think of our pleasant old village, and its quiet, shady street, and consider the desolation that might come to it, turn from the gifts which the interlopers bring to us, and ask instead, " Beauty for ashes, the oil of joy for mourning, the garment of praise for the spirit of heaviness."

AUGUST 3, 1894.

XLI.

At last! at last!—

The thirsty earth soaks up the rain,
And drinks, and gapes for drink again.

For some days there has been an increasing thickening in the atmosphere, and a greater frequency in the storms which come to naught. But day by day passed by, and the dry grasses hung their dispirited blades in the face of high heaven. As from time to time we saw the rain falling upon the distant hills, or heard of the refreshing showers in the neighbouring towns, we began to wonder with them of old (it seems to me that I remember some such passage), " Were they wicked above all others upon whom the tower in Siloam fell?" and were we wicked above all others upon whom the rain did not fall?

Yester evening as I left the hillside, my builder pointed out this and that sign in the lowering sky which augured well for the morrow. But when I sought my downy

couch, faint stars still glimmered in the
quiet night.

Midnight was not long past, however,
before a steady pattering on the maple
leaves outside the window recalled me
from the land of No-whither into which I
had sunk. Had I but learned to "dream
true," I think that I should not have re-
turned so easily, even upon so pleasant a
call. But alas! I have not yet acquired
that faculty, though I mean to do so one
of these days. As it was, the sound was
balm to my spirit, and I lay for a long time
listening to the pleasant dropping, and
grudging to fall asleep again lest I should
waste a pleasant opportunity, and somehow, by carelessness, bring the shower to
an end. And so I continued waking and
sleeping, waking and sleeping, through the
night, keeping watch and ward over the
elements, and congratulating myself in an
incoherent way that the liquid chain did
not break.

The rain continued pretty steadily until
the middle of the morning, when occasional
flashes of lightning and rumbling of distant thunder told us that we had to do
with an electric storm, and not with a full-
grown north-easter. And then the last

drops were wrung out, the expanding cir-
cles ceased upon the pools, the rivulets ran
away from the newly stratified sand upon
the roadways, with their wave lines and
curves and ripples, and through a rift in
the gray clouds the sun poured down its
golden rays again upon the grass field,
already showing a fresh verdancy after the
unwonted refreshment.

The world goes up, and the world goes down,
And the sunshine follows the rain.

It is the first time in many, many weeks
that the ground has been soaked, and I do
not mourn over the deep pools in my cellar,
or begin to speculate upon the probability
of my being able to establish a domestic
trout pond in that convenient locality. I
merely realize gratefully that there is
scarcely a physical possibility that we shall
have it so dry again before the frost comes.

Some others of our home circle are gone,
soon to return, we hope, with the shortening days and lengthening nights, these to
the Narragansett shore, and those to the
rocks of the Pine Tree State. And to-morrow Monsieur and Madame Liquidambar
tempt the ocean surges in quest of the

green lanes and ivy-mantled towers of
Merrie England, and of the lakes and
mountains of misty Scotland. I wonder
whether mayhap in some al fresco repast
at Melrose or Dryburgh, or on Ellen's
Isle, they may taste the

> Herbs, and other country messes,
> Which the neat-handed Phillis dresses.

But the Scribe clings to his hillside, and
as again in the darkness of the deepening night the fountains of the heavens are
opened, and empty themselves upon the
earth, he gratefully realizes the blessings
of the present, and would fain believe
that "contentment is better than wealth,"
and home more kindly than "abroad."

Not that in imagination he does not see

> The cloud-capped towers, the gorgeous pal-
> aces,
> The solemn temples,

which he would dearly like to view in
visible presence; not that he would not
tread with reverent awe the aisles worn
by the weary feet of unnumbered generations seeking a disentanglement of the
insoluble riddle of life. Not that he does
not esteem a certain discontent the main-

spring of progress, and the hope of the race.

But to the beatific vision which solicits him with beckoning hand, he points to the unfinished cottage upon the hillside, shows duties to be performed, and obstacles which cannot be surmounted.   And accepting the decree of the gods, he looks fondly upon valley, hills, and sky, and to the vision he saith : —

> Ask me no more: the moon may draw the
>   sea ;
> The cloud may stoop from heaven and take
>   the shape,
> With fold to fold, of mountain or of cape ;
> But, O too fond, when have I answered thee ?
>   Ask me no more.

AUGUST 4, 1894.

XLII.

O Tannenbaum, O Tannenbaum,
Wie treu sind Deine Blätter.

A GOOD straight cedar tree stands upon
the end of the ridge-pole of the cottage. It
was planted there yesterday afternoon in
token of the fact that the summit had been
reached, the place of the dividing of the
waters, not the sweet vale of Avoca. At
length the bones are in place, and ready to
be clothed upon with the membranes which
are to give a seeming of continuity and
bodily substance to the structure.

We can now see the outline in its general
character, and are able to judge as to its fit-
ness for the location, and are called upon
to decide whether the building improves or
desecrates the position which it occupies.
I fear that this is a consideration all too
seldom taken into account. In this instance,
so far as expressed, opinions coincide, and
for myself I am quite content. Nature takes
kindly to her bosom the newcomer, which

seems at the beginning in good measure a
real part of herself, not a jarring note: promising to become rapidly a true flower of the
landscape, and not a blot upon it, as I am
afraid that the majority of American houses
are.

And speaking of flowers, I wish that you
could see the glory in lace and purple and
gold of my pasture, which I look down upon
between the unclothed ribs of the building.
Upon the upper portion, near the woods, a
great bed of the richly-hued ironweed ex-
ceeds in beauty, I think, any that I ever
saw before, while mingled somewhat with
it and spread more fully over the body
of the field, the wild carrot lifts its stately
jewels, and the golden-rod is beginning to
hang out its graceful plumes.   In the marsh
at the foot the intense green is beginning to
be sprinkled with the white flowers of the
sagittaria and the grass of Parnassus, while
the wild clematis twines gracefully over the
heaps of stones, and the rich clusters of the
elderberries hang nodding in the hedgerows.   The rose-hips are beginning to show
an orange tinge, and here and there over
the slope dark young cedars lift themselves
above the tall " weeds " and grass.

On the other side of the house, the undulating mountain meadow is being ploughed up after many years' rest, shortly to be seeded down again to grass for firm sod and mowing. If all goes well, I should next June look from the triple window in my living room across a smooth, unbroken sea of waving spires to the line of the southern hills, cut only by the elm and locust trees upon the roadside five hundred feet away.

The katydids are here. Only for two evenings have I noticed them, but during those two, they have filled the air with the iteration of their calls. With the same persistence as a year ago, they keep up the charge and denial, appearing in fact to have gained force and volume during the year that has passed.

The days grow shorter, and it seems as if the fall were fast approaching. The sky is overcast, and after the heat of July the air seems chill, and a grateful fire smoulders upon the hearth at the inn. But the burning sun will doubtless scorch us yet for many days, ere the woods turn scarlet and brown and gold, and the wanderers return from their journeyings.

AUGUST 12, 1894.

XLIII.

Has it ever occurred to you how purely
conventional, arbitrary, and false are our
ordinary views of business and occupation?
I will not say that the money test is the sole
one which is applied, but those which sup-
plement it are usually much of the same
character. Undoubtedly the first consideration for all, is the maintenance of life, for,
as it is held on the border that the only
good Indian is a dead Indian, so *e converso*,
it is felt, I suppose, by each of us, that we
can be of precious little service unless we
are alive. Of course, in the case of many,
this impression could be effectually con-
tested, and of such it could be proved that
nothing in their lives became them so well
as would their leaving of them. But speaking generally, the keeping of the breath in
the body is the primary object of each, and
the effort to do this accounts in a large
measure for the subserviency in a mercan-
tile world to the test referred to. I was led
to reflect upon this subject at the moment

by recalling what a vast number of persons
there are, especially in the cities, who, having already acquired sufficient means for a
comfortable livelihood for themselves and
their families, and having no great taste for
the spectacular in living, or enjoyment in it,
yet keep on from year to year in the old
tread-mill round, because they or their
friends think that they ought not to " retire from business." Some of them are
old, some middle-aged, and some are young.
Some have inherited a comfortable compe-
tency and never have needed to earn money.
But they must continue in " business";
they are too young to "retire." It does
not seem to make any difference what the
business is. It may be useful, it may be in-
different, it may be positively harmful to the
community, — still it is business. It may be
something which no one else could do so
well, or something requiring a capacity pos-
sessed by those of whom " the woods are
full," who are only waiting for a break in
the line to rush into the place.

Without entering upon the question of
the relative importance of necessaries and
luxuries, which in its essence is largely a
question of tastes and desires sound in
themselves, and of a breadth or narrowness

of view as to what a well-developed, well-rounded life requires — it may safely be said that a very large percentage of the business of the world is deleterious to its welfare, and detrimental to the progress of the race ; that those engaged in such business, which may be their sole, or only a part of their occupation, are stumbling-blocks in the upward march. It is hardly necessary to particularize ; in some directions each will involuntarily draw a line under certain familiar occupations. But leaving aside the obvious instances, it is sufficient to touch lightly only one or two spots, to show what I mean. I suppose that there are very few thoughtful, intelligent men even in the journalistic fraternity itself, who would not agree that it would be better that a vast proportion of all the work done in connection with the newspaper press, by editors, reporters, telegraph operators, compositors, printers' devils, distributors, in short. by all hands, should be left undone ; that if such were the case the world would be richer, wiser, and saner than it is to-day. So likewise with the general publishing business, though possibly, probably, not to so large a degree. The same may be said, *mutatis mutandis*, of many other occupations. Yet all these things are business, and so long as a man is engaged in any one of them, he is popularly supposed to be a useful member of society, while if he has "retired," he has ceased to be such, and has become as it were simply as a "fifth wheel to a coach."

Now, in the last analysis, nothing could be more absurd than this. The only solid basis which the idea rests upon, is just the one which, practically, is wholly left out of the account. That is, that in a social world, each should do a portion of the world's necessary work, and this according to his ability to do it, and not necessarily for pay, or because he needs the pay which may be given for it. If the work which he does is not a part of the work which helps the world along, it is useless work, however much he may be paid for it; and if the work is something which does help the world along, even in the least degree, it is part of the true world's work, even if it be anything but what is ordinarily called business, and even if the suggestion that it had a money value would excite a shout of derision from the thoughtless all over the land. Indeed, it might belong in one of these categories and yet be absolutely priceless.

As an unmistakable example of what I mean, to put an extreme case and yet an impregnable one, I should say that he or she who can by spirit and demeanour bring a warm throb to the heart and a tremulous smile to the lips of those sad or crusty ones who are met in the course of the day, is one whose price is above rubies.

Now be it remembered that I am speaking of those who do not need to toil to earn a subsistence or comforts, but who still remain in the familiar harness, and their name may be said to be legion. It is fair to assume that a large proportion of them are engaged in fairly useful employments. In the case of most of these, should they leave their present occupations, their places would be immediately filled by the pressure from below, the world's work would go on as well as ever, and many would be benefited. Are they then to do nothing? Not so. The world has enough work for all hands to do, and the farthest vision cannot see a state where the same may not truly be said. As society is organized, it is impossible to place a money value upon much of this work, which is of the most necessary character, and if it is to be done well, it must be done gratuitously or without a material return by those whose hearts are in it. Much time cannot be given it by those who are engaged in business, because in business the rules require the rigour of the game, and inattention to these rules very surely must be followed by its loss. It is therefore peculiarly the work for those from whom the burden of care for their personal future has been removed.

The most obvious side of the work to which I allude is the work which concerns the public welfare, and this has many branches; the next is that which concerns those individuals who have in a certain sense been forgotten. In each direction the field is so broad as to leave room for the imagination to expand indefinitely, and I might leave it to each to follow out for himself the thread of thought suggested, in the direction most congenial to him. Perhaps I may feel moved to indicate some special lines of activity and helpfulness which come into my view. But does it not appear to you that the world might soon be a very different world from the one we know, if an earnest effort should be made in the direction which I have indicated? And remember that I am not suggesting a distasteful, laborious change of occupation, but a choice of activity upon congenial lines. As I said some time ago, find out in which way the eternal stream is flowing, and row with the current.

AUGUST 12, 1894.

Q

XLIV.

THE day is warm, and it is a trial to walk along the hot and dusty road; the distant hills float and fade in the soft haze; but sitting here at the carpenter's bench in my bay window and looking southward, a refreshing breeze tempers the heat, and though the currents in the fervid air rising from the newly ploughed field cause a flickering in the outlines of objects near the surface, suggestive of a seven-times-heated furnace, at a little greater height and distance the finger-like motions to and fro of the pendulous branches of slender elms, and the multitudinous ripple on the surface of dense maples and velvety locust trees, give a sense of life and healthfulness. Here and there the tops of chokecherries and other shrubs peering above the curve of the rolling field, and now and then the upper rail and the posts of a few panels of fence, indicate the line of the highway, but, fortunately, no unsightly telegraph poles

break the line of the horizon or otherwise
destroy the unity and beauty of the scene.

I wonder if Jeremiah was considered a
common scold. I think that the avocation
of a common scold must be classed among
the most praiseworthy. That is, if it be
possible by any means to awaken the æsthetic sense in a people given over to a
crass barbarism. This morning I walked
for a mile or so along the highway, from
which almost anywhere, excepting where
recent grading had shut it in between high
banks, an outlook could be had upon scenes
beautiful enough to shame any but the
most callous. Along the way, sometimes
together and sometimes opposed to each
other, ran two lines of telegraph poles,
rough, bare, crooked trunks, carrying numerous wires, and to these has been added
another row for the trolley system, carrying two great cables in addition to the
bright copper conducting wire. The incongruity with the landscape was shocking,
the disfigurement atrocious. And the road
itself had a bed formed of imperfect or dis-
integrating red sandstone, a sort of hardpan, rough and yet dusty, with irregularly
gashed banks, and no footway on either
side. Is this worthy of a civilized people?

I remember reading somewhere an article in which the writer accounted for the small amount of walking done by our people, by the absence of good footpaths along our roads and through our fields. And, inadequate as the reason may appear to some of us, who were born with legs and were taught in childhood how to use them, it is a reason which has weight, and a reason which should not be allowed to exist. The fact is an evidence of our imperfect development, but it is a fact, that with comparative infrequency do we find a comfortable path along any of our ordinary country roads. He or she who goes from house to house or from village to village on foot, which most have to do at times, and all ought often to do, is compelled to take to the dusty wagon track, or to scramble up and down rough banks and among the vines and bushes and weeds. The vines and bushes and weeds are not to blame. They often form the chief beauty of the roadside, until some enterprising farmer or road mender comes along and cuts and hacks until he has left nothing but a barren waste, naught but short stumps projecting above prostrate saplings and seedlings, upon which the unripe leaves wilt and turn brown and rattle in the hot wind.

No, we do not need that the rich growth of the roadside should be shorn away, or that the banks should be graded like city sidewalks and planked or paved. What we want is a simple, practicable way among the bushes beside the road ; so located as to avoid unnecessary jumping and climbing, and to be protected from washing by storm currents. And for the path itself, the foot of the passer may be relied upon in most cases to establish that, provided the way be given. The proverb goes, that for him who wears shoes all the world is covered with leather, or words to that effect ; and this leather, or even bare feet, if there be enough of them, will soon make upon a sound sod as good a path as one could wish.

So much for the highways ; but should we always be confined to these ? A man's house is, and undoubtedly should be, his castle, and undoubtedly each has a right to insist upon his own privacy. But this right has its limitations. I always resent the placarding of large tracts with " Trespassing forbidden," when merely walking over the fields is assumed to be trespass. At many points along the seashore now, it is almost impossible for the stranger to dip his hand into the salt sea waves, or even to come into plain sight of the mighty deep. And in some of our inland regions it is almost as bad, or it would be, could owners accomplish what they frequently attempt. There is something very human in the old-world prescriptive easements, which preserve to the public the right of way over private property by definite paths. How vastly the pleasure of country saunterings is thereby increased, to say nothing of the convenience of the wayfarer! That property suffers in any way thereby, I do not understand to be the case. I have been interested in some discussion in " Garden and Forest," of the use of paths versus the common use of the meadows in public parks. I am strongly of the opinion that the editor is right in the position that for most people the paths to walk upon, and the sod to look upon, afford the essentials of enjoyment. Doubtless all wish occasionally to feel the turf beneath them. Doubtless also there is something in individual bent, and something in age which must be considered. I note that for myself, I keep more to the beaten paths than I used to do. It is said that with advancing years there is a more and more pronounced lack of the earlier flexibility in the joints. But how should *we* know?

Be that as it may, I am sure that a proper provision of paths through private lands, with turnstiles, gates, or bars where necessary, would contribute vastly to the comfort and enjoyment of the public, and would not be to the detriment of the private owners. I am strongly inclined to believe that we should be better off, if the right to use such paths should inure to the public as an indefeasible right, as in the cases that I have mentioned; but without insisting upon this, it is quite safe to say, that he who offers to his neighbours the privilege of such enjoyment of his domain, shows that so far forth, at least, he has become a civilized man.

August 19, 1894.

XLV.

A SHORT time ago I had something to say upon the matter of population, and the assumed value of a dense population, a most singular and elaborate piece of self-deception. It is, I suppose, a natural, though even in that case, a questionable policy, which animates the West in encouraging immigration, for with native resources greatly in excess of the demands upon them, a greater density in population may aid in promoting prosperity and physical — in some cases even mental and spiritual, well-being. But in the more fully occupied Eastern states this is much more rarely the case : in many places it is not so in any sense, and in the cities the contrary is so, with great emphasis. The tendency to congregate in the cities is notorious, and this makes our municipal problems the most serious with which we have to deal.

There has been in the past much controversy over the contention of Malthus that population tends to increase with greater rapidity than material resources; yet I cannot see but that in its essence it is impregnable. The tendency is practically more or less held in check, but mainly by misery and disease. And in this connection, this is to be noted: that as a general rule, — of course with numerous exceptions, — the higher in the grade of civilization, the fewer the offspring, — the lower, the more prolific. The consequences of this tendency are most marked. The frequency with which families which have been publicly known for several generations, die out and disappear, is notorious. The small number of individuals in such of these families as continue, is as familiar. On the other hand, the magnitude of the families of those who have small resources, and whose demands, though considerable, are within a narrow range, is patent to every one. There is a constant tendency in our society to die at the top — a constant tendency toward a dominance of the lower stratum, which tendency, as I have before said, is chiefly checked — at present — by misery and disease.

There are several manifest causes for this condition of things, and perhaps other causes which are not so evident, — doubtless some which we do not recognize. On the part of the well-to-do, or those who make similar demands upon life because of the character of their education or for certain social reasons, there is undoubtedly, in the first place, less of the simply animal; then there are usually much later marriages; and, in the third place, there is a very considerable amount of deliberate prudence. On the part of the poor and uneducated on the other hand. there is undoubtedly greater fecundity accompanying a closer acclimation, as it were, to the conditions in which they are placed; there are much earlier marriages; and there is apparently no restraint at all upon their numerous increase: with each one it is "Happy is the man that hath his quiver full," — until he finds that in his case the saying should read, "Unhappy is the man."

Now the trouble is that as among the thoughtless poor, only necessity restricts the growth of population, as a rule, any sudden development of prosperity unaccompanied by a significant enlightenment, is pretty sure to be followed by a more rapid increase in population, and therefore in the demands upon the physical resources. The spasm of prosperity dies away; the increased population is left to struggle for subsistence, with diminished means.

The most acute investigators, especially in the great cities, and notably in London, have found no question half so difficult to deal with as this. Penniless boys marry before they can earn a livelihood for themselves, and the most unsavoury and unwholesome dens teem like ant-hills. What is to be done about it? Well, it is hard to say what can be done about it, farther than to use every effort to destroy this wild theory of which I have been writing, that a numerous population is a good thing in itself, and to instil into the minds of the struggling poor the importance of self-control and later marriages.

We have heard a good deal of the efforts of the Anti Poverty Society in New York, —a crusade as absurd and as futile in the manner in which it was undertaken as anything ever devised by Don Quixote. I am not sure that in the present prosperous condition of the world (I do not mean prosperous condition of "business"; "business" is not prosperous) there is any necessity for poverty. I am sure that, if the age at marriage could be raised by ten years among the very poor and the people of moderate means, and the number of children hereafter born decreased by one-half, there would no longer be any necessity for poverty, excepting on the ground of gross incapacity ; but, on the contrary, within a generation the " workingman " would find prosperity at his beck and call.

AUGUST 19, 1894.

XLVI.

I SEE that Lord Salisbury, in his address as president before the British Association for the Advancement of Science, takes occasion to speak at length of the things which we do not know, — a very wholesome reminder, and much needed by many people. I fear that the rapid discovery of details in regard to methods of growth and development, during late years, has produced an undue feeling of extensive and comprehensive and commanding knowledge on the part of the unthinking, not at all allied to a cautious modesty. These things are enormously interesting and important, and it is a source of great regret to me to find so many people whose eyes have not been opened to them, and whose time occasionally hangs heavy on their hands — time which, under other circumstances, would be filled to repletion with the joy of living and knowing.

But, after all, the startling, the appalling thing is, not the extent of what we know, but the extent of that which we do not

know. I find " I don't know " the household words most familiar in my mouth.
" As our little life is rounded with a sleep,"
so our little knowledge is rounded with an
illimitable ocean of nescience. Moreover,
it is well to remember that much of that
which we call knowledge, much of that
which is classed as " science " to-day, is
here and there founded upon hypotheses,
admirable for a working basis, but subject
to modification, or rejection, as investigation progresses. For many people it is very
difficult to remember this, and they are
apt to talk and act as if there were conditions of positiveness about that which
is oftentimes merely tentative. So long
as a theory will explain all the known
facts, it is a good theory; the moment a
discovery is made of something for which
it does not account, it falls to pieces like
a house of cards. And our knowledge, so
far as we have it, is relative : this, that, and
the other, stand in a certain proportion and
connection with each other ; beyond is the
infinite gulf, — we are suspended in mid-
air. For the ancients, the world rested
upon the back of an elephant, and the elephant stood upon a tortoise : the tortoise
upon what ?

To-day, our notions are clearer, but we are met by precisely the same problem, and I am inclined to think that we shall be so met forever. We no longer think of the elephant and the tortoise, but of the globe swinging in ether, with innumerable other globes, bound together and kept apart by the attraction of gravitation and certain specified motions. But, as Lord Salisbury says, what is the ether? and also what is gravitation, and what is beyond the limits of the myriad orbs?

Did it ever occur to you that the ultimate things, the only things which are impregnable facts, the things that must be, are for the human mind, unthinkable, or inconceivable, except as a form of words? It has been customary to criticise severely the attitude of mind of him who says, "I believe, because it is impossible," and I wholly agree with the ordinary application of this criticism. And yet, after all, the greatest things, the outlying and unalterable facts, which are not affected by hypothesis, and which we are bound to accept, are impossible, in our thought. Take, for example, two of the most important, time and space. There are, so far as I can conceive, but two alternatives in regard to each of these. Either there was a beginning of time, or there was no beginning; either there will be an end of time, or there will be no end. So with space: either there is a point beyond which there is nothing — not even vacancy — or there is no such point.

Now our minds refuse to accept either time or space with a limit beyond which it does not extend. They ask forever, What is beyond? In like manner, they refuse to accept anything which is interminable. Even a future state of existence, which goes on and on, and yet again on, becomes a horror to thought, if dwelt upon, not only because the feeling of change and rest is sweet, but because we are bound to ask, When will the end come? And what comes after the end? We look into space and can neither imagine a limit beyond which the line cannot extend, nor can we imagine unlimited extension of the line. Why, then, do we properly feel satisfied that certain things are facts, and chide him who says, "I believe, because it is impossible"? Because in the field of relative knowledge which we have investigated, we have accumulated a vast hoard of antecedents and consequents, which we have formulated into what we call laws of nature, and it is in this field that we are

most apt to find the loose thinking and
superstition which we are compelled to criticise. But here again caution is most com-
mendable. A law of man is a rule imposed
from without. A law of nature is simply
our formulation of the order of events as we
find them in nature. The evidence at our
disposal may be little, or it may be great;
the law may be firmly established by an
invariable sequence of occurrences through
the course of ages, or it may depend upon
a few observations within a limited field, and
may be subject to modifications upon fuller
and more extensive observation. Andrew
Lang and Professor Huxley seem to have
come into collision in a case of this kind,
and we cannot but feel that in this case the
literary man has, in a degree, the better of
the scientific man, in that his attitude of
mind under the circumstances is more in
accordance with the temper of a philosophic
investigator, however ignorant he may be as
compared with his opponent relative to the
matter in hand.

> There are more things in heaven and **earth,**
>   Horatio,
> Than are dreamt of in your philosophy.

Professor Huxley seems to have forgotten

R

for the moment what was clear to the poet, and seems to an outsider to exhibit a little too much cocksureness.

The prevailing philosophy of the time is the evolution philosophy of Herbert Spencer, brilliantly illustrated, in a part of its field, by the observations and demonstrations of Charles Darwin upon biological questions in regard to the origin and development of species. Mr. Spencer's theory harmonizes with the great mass of facts which have been accumulated through the ages, and the grasp of his mind is so great, and the extent of his labours has been so enormous, that he has compelled the admiration and enthusiastic devotion of a large number of our scientific men. You remember what Matthew Prior says: —

> Be to her virtues very kind ;
> Be to her faults a little blind.

This we are bound to do in regard to Mr. Spencer, but, on the other hand, we ought to remember that in the nature of things, a stupendous work such as that which Mr. Spencer is engaged upon is bound to contain errors, and the ready recognition of this fact would be a safer attitude on the part of those of us who feel ourselves his disciples, rather than an unquestioning acceptance of everything that he writes. Moreover, may I not as a Spencerian pupil safely say that it is too early to claim more, for much of Mr. Spencer's philosophy, than that it is a good, an admirable working hypothesis, but still an hypothesis? For myself, I may say that it is the grandest that ever opened before my vision, and that it fills my mind and heart with an awe and a reverence for the all-comprehending, all-inspiring mystic essence which is at the heart of things, which are unspeakable.

But it is this incomprehensible mystery,

A motion and a spirit, that impels
All thinking things, all objects of all thought,
And rolls through all things,

that is the final incontrovertible fact, not anything hitherto formulated regarding it.

SEPTEMBER 2, 1894.

XLVII.

In one of my earlier notes I referred to those who refuse to interest themselves in the details of the structure and life of plants and other objects about them, and quietly scoffed at their apparent fear lest the mystery of life should be wholly explained, and nothing be left to wonder at or reverence. And I have just enforced this thought at greater length, and tried to show that at the best we are but as bits of floating down, surrounded by an unfathomable and incomprehensible immensity.

Yet for the practical man of affairs, and woman of society whose attention has not been drawn to the larger questions, but who have been alive to the surface changes, there is a certain partial excuse for this attitude of mind in the events of the past century, and especially of the past fifty years.

The material progress of the world since the close of the American and the French revolutions, the development of invention with the resulting changes in methods and manner of living and extent of intercourse, the close observation of occurrences and the analysis of processes, the co-ordination of the results of this observation and analysis, and the deductions therefrom, have combined to make an era unique in the world's history, and which we cannot imagine as continuing at the same rate of progress for another hundred years, without something akin to vertigo.

This is the *fin de siècle;* and I suppose that we are all its children, with all that that implies. The year 1900 is close upon us. It is a pertinent inquiry, therefore, what the twentieth century will bring to us. Will our great cities increase in the next hundred years in the same ratio as in the past; and will the enemies of private ownership of land have succeeded in what seems to be their darling project, — in so controlling public affairs as to induce the building over of all the breathing-places in these cities, so far happily kept out of the market? If so, we must be prepared for a great cockney population, whose sole knowledge of the country and of plant life, if they be readers, will be drawn from history and current literature, and if they be of the class of non-readers, which class such a life must largely increase, must be derived from the clothes poles with pulleys in back yards, surrounded by ragged walls, with purslane and plantains scattered over the ground between, or from the wilted vegetables at the corner grocery.

Another hundred years of manufacturing at the present rate of development, according to careful computers, will exhaust the supply of coal available at any reasonable cost, and a much shorter period, the valuable timber. One of three things: either the rate of development must greatly diminish, or second, our manufactories and our railroads must come to a halt, or third, some form of power now unused, or used but to a small extent, must take the place of that now derived from the consumption of coal and wood.

There are three great storehouses still at our disposal, and largely unused: that of the sun, that of the air, and that of the water. Ericsson experimented with the first with great burning glasses, with indeterminate, though, I think, rather hopeful results. The probability of success in this direction depends largely upon the period of the year, and upon the climate.

Success is most likely in the tropics, though I think Underledge would have afforded an especially promising field during the past summer.

The wind has, in one way or other, been harnessed to the chariot of progress since the earliest time upon the sea, and through many generations upon the land. It is in the latter direction that we must expect most progress to be made in the future. Let us hope that the coming windmill will not be such a blot upon the landscape as those with which we have been afflicted during the past half-century. I suppose that we cannot expect anything so pictur-esque as the old mill of Holland.

Lastly we come to the water. Probably the waters that come down at Lodore, as well as those of Niagara, the falls of Min-nehaha and of Montmorency, and all the sublime and beautiful torrents that have inspired art or literature, must ultimately turn some one's mill wheel. But all the power of the accessible streams combined, is of small account when compared with that stored up or available in the ocean tides. Everywhere upon our eastern shore bears the mass of the Atlantic. On the west we have the Pacific, and on the south the Gulf of Mexico. Four times each day these immense bodies of water are pouring upon us, or away from us, as the sun and the moon tug at the earth in opposition or together. Here are, let us say, more than three thousand miles of coast-line, to say nothing of the rivers in which the tide rises and falls, upon which the tides move with a height varying from a few inches up to forty feet or more. In how many places this power is now used, I cannot say — probably but few. I know an old tide mill on Sheepshead Bay, on the south shore of Long Island, a favourite destination for a canter or trot in the old times, which always interested me ; but it is the only one I ever saw.

Now, that either or all three of these great sources of power can be drawn upon to an enormous extent to stimulate electrical energy, which seems likely to be the immediate agent of the future for the distribution of force, I take it that there can be no reasonable doubt. It is simply a question of gearing and application, a matter for inventors to play with, and the American inventor will disappoint just expectation if he does not succeed in surmounting the difficulties which manifest themselves at the outset.

But reliance upon either of these sources rather than upon fuel, implies great changes in methods, — I hope that we may believe changes for the better, at least in some respects. Let us pray that it may produce a tendency toward a decentralization of population, and this we have a right to hope. The human being is a social being, and he not only likes, but he needs society for his proper development. But there are degrees of intimacy, different grades of nearness in social relations, as there are in expressions of disapproval.

> Perhaps it was right to dissemble your love,
> But — why did you kick me down stairs?

You can have all the company that is good for you without continually touching elbows with your neighbours upon either side.

The question of the extent and character of the mechanical power in use, is one of the greatest questions affecting mankind, as I have heretofore intimated, and, as I have ventured also to assert, its increase is not an unmixed benefit. I can imagine the tone of the race as becoming higher, while the proportionate weight of mechanical power in use becomes less, although I would not say that this is a necessary relation. Human development depends for the most part upon mental stimulus, and though probably greater productiveness results from the present tendency to enormous aggregations of workers under comparatively few " Captains of Industry," I question whether this tendency does not check mental activity with many. And mental breadth is undoubtedly circumscribed by too great a division of labour. The extent to which this is now carried is astonishing, and I was much struck a few days ago by the statement made to me by a friend, upon his return from one of our hill towns, of the manner in which this has even affected farmers of late years, through the introduction of the creamery and other establishments and methods of co-operation. The saving virtue in this particular instance is the enormous relief afforded to the housewife.

I find that I have been beguiled into a consideration especially of the recent and prospective changes in material conditions. But these are closely connected with revolutionary changes in theology, philosophy, science, and art, all of which are in a ferment, in a chaotic condition, which forbids close prophecy. A friend recently said to me that it would be interesting to know what we, or those that shall follow us, will be thinking, fifty or sixty years hence. It would indeed ; but a thick veil shrouds the future. Probably the most that we can say is, that the past, and many of the ideas of the past, are gone, and forever. The latter were legitimate children of their time, and they doubtless served their purpose, but they are out of key with our larger view, and no power exists by which they can be revivified. We seem to see some stable ground emerging from the troubled waters of the present, but all that we can certainly say, is, that whatever of vesture fades and vanishes, the eternal verities remain the same yesterday, to-day, and forever ; and the time-spirit saith : —

Here at the whirring loom of time I sit and
   ply,
And weave for God the garment thou dost
   see him by.

SEPTEMBER 2, 1894.

XLVIII.

Water, water, everywhere,
Nor any drop to drink.

IF we could only say so much as that,
we should feel fairly well pleased. We
remember sympathetically the little girl in
the story, who, when she heard that some
neighbours had no bread to eat, expressed
her wonder that they did not then eat cake,
and we should try to get along bravely with
some other beverage. But, alas! it is not
" water, water everywhere." A month ago
I recorded a refreshing rain, continuing for
several hours, and I congratulated myself
that there was scarcely a physical possibility
that we should have it so dry again before
the time of frost. But since then the drought
has once more settled down upon us, and we
have not had enough of a shower to lay the
dust. In the morning a fog covers the valley, and during the day a canopy of smoke
and haze covers the heavens, through which
the sun sometimes glows like a ball of red-

hot iron, at which one can look without
flinching.

Only once has the smoke fallen low
enough for me to perceive its odour, and
this was at nightfall a few days ago, as I
drove over the hills some miles to the westward of the village. Yesterday in the afternoon, I suddenly perceived a flame on the
side of the mountain two or three miles to
the northeastward, but it lasted but a little
while, and I presume was looked after and
taken care of by vigilant watchers. This
afternoon the atmosphere thickened until
the sun wholly disappeared, and with it
most of the landscape, and people spoke of
the famous "yellow day," although the
colour was not so marked as it has been on
two or three occasions during the past
week; but the barometer is high, and
mounts steadily higher.

My strawberry plants, which took a good
hold on the earth, are dying one by one,
and half are gone. But the melons seem
to revel in the dry soil and heavy air, from
which they have somehow extracted the
most delicious juices, while my tomatoes
and corn and potatoes defy competitors
through all the countryside. It should be
said, however, that we have had heavy dews,

and I suppose that this accounts for the vegetation that has been saved. But since the sower went forth to sow my grass field, I desire something better.

The search for water leads me to the well, and this, alas! is still marked with an interrogation point. The permanent pump has been put in place and finds a continuous supply. But the supply, though gratefully cool and refreshing to the taste, has still the colour of *café au lait*, and seems to promise a richness which is uncalled for. The interesting question which the future is asked to solve is whether we have struck a quicksand, and if so, whether we shall have to pump out a deposit of some thousands of cubic yards before we attain a clear and wholesome beverage.

Down in the marsh the water still stands here and there between the tussocks of coarse grass, notwithstanding the long drought, and on the margin of the meadow there is an unmistakable spring, where the frogs make merry. In an experimental way, therefore, I have begun digging, with the hope of forming a series of small pools, in which pond lilies may float, while cardinal flowers and marshmallows and other denizens of the low lands make gay the border.

I would that I had a mountain brook, brawling over the stones on the ledge, and gliding through the meadow, but for this I fear that I must look to the winter alone.

SEPTEMBER 2, 1894.

XLIX.

HIGHER and higher rose the barometer, and denser and denser became the atmosphere, until the valley nearly disappeared and the heavens were covered by a leaden veil. Yesterday we had seen some indications of a mackerel sky beyond the smoke, and at last, shortly before noon to-day, first in tiny particles at long intervals, and then more frequently, the moisture made itself felt, until at length a real shower was sweeping over the fields. Now we were sure that the September rains had begun in earnest, and those that were upon the housetop came down, and those who were in the fields sought shelter. But alas! the shower was but a fleeting show: it had but little more than moistened the surface, when it was gone.

Slight as it was, however, the effect upon the atmosphere was wonderful. The smoke had disappeared; the sky was cobalt blue once more, for the first time in weeks, and the sun poured down a hot torrent upon us.

I noticed a curious effect, such as might easily have given rise to a wholly false impression. The rain had not been falling more than five minutes, when behold the brown and newly seeded field was sprinkled over with spires of green grass from two to four inches in height. It seemed like the marvellous tricks of the Oriental conjurors, who are said to plant a seed, develop a tree, and produce the fruit while you wait.

Now I have no doubt that this grass had sprung up from the overturned sod, and that it was all standing in the field ere the rain began, but coated over with a fine powder of dust, which the falling drops washed away, leaving the field, though sparsely, in verdure clad. Thus often the senses deceive us, and false testimony may unwittingly be given by the best-intentioned.

It is pleasant to see the blue once more, pleasant to catch a glimpse of the distant hills, even if here and there we observe that the finger of autumn has already touched the trees and left a blush of crimson or a golden glow upon them ; pleasant also is it this evening to see the friendly moon and stars once more lending their light to cheer the night hours.

And through the clearer air comes to me a soft little blossom of the Edelweiss, plucked close to the snow on the Breithorn, a fortnight ago. Yes, perhaps it is peculiar; but it is nevertheless a brave survivor of "the slings and arrows of outrageous fortune," and though it may come from the very shadow of the eternal snows, I am sure it brings to me a little warmth of kindly human feeling in its heart.

SEPTEMBER 6, 1894.

L.

At last Polyphemus is here; the great one-eyed monster that has taken possession of our highway, and bound it with iron bars. An authority tells us that Polyphemus "fed upon human flesh, and kept his flocks upon the coasts of Sicily." We might have known as much. The other Sicilians were here a month ago, as I remarked at the time, and alas! we be very much afeared that the monster's appetite is still unsated, and that human flesh will yet have to be sacrificed to him. But Galatea shall be secluded, if it be possible.

What a terror that glaring eye will be for many a day to man and woman and beast, as the car speeds its way through the night along the common highway. With a rattle and a whizz and a rush; with the sulphurous looking sparks flying from overhead as the revolving trolley makes and breaks connections, the heavy vehicle bowls away, bearing its human freight through the darkness along the dusty road, stirring the damp and heavy air, and startling crickets and katydids from their monotonous and unending conversations, while the occasional glow-worm by the roadside, in proportion to his weight, outdoes the giant in his illumination.

Polyphemus is here, for weal or for woe. When man makes a scar on the hillside, a great grey or brown scar, where sand and pebbles and clay drift down in ridges, and the rain water cuts channels between, after a while along come the moss and the cinque-foil, the chamomile, the asters, and the golden-rod, and then the white birches, and heal the scar and clothe it and bring it back into harmony with nature as a part of the land of the living. Perhaps, somehow, this blot which marks our pristine freshness may be turned to wholesome uses, and the path of the monster may yet be embroidered with flowers of the Spirit.

SEPTEMBER 6, 1894.

LI.

It droppeth as the gentle rain from heaven
Upon the place beneath.

COULD any simile produce a more definite and wholly satisfying picture upon the mind ? All through the morning the words have been singing themselves to me as I worked under shelter with saw and chisel, hammer and nails. securely placing the new foster mother which is to brood over the coming generation of foundlings in my poultry yard. Now more slowly, and now faster, the light patter sounded upon the roof ; the little fluffy bipeds without shook and stretched themselves, and sought shelter from a dispensation to which they were unused, and the clean white elders gathered about and dabbled in a muddy pool which had quickly formed. Corn blades and grass blades glistened after their bath, and the dry earth of the newly tilled field eagerly drank up the welcome drops, for which the grass seed had been waiting for a week.

And I hoped that far away in the woods, the rain might overtake the fell destroyer on his fiery path, and quietly smother his rage, even as balm may sometime light upon the hearts of those whose homes and hearths he has already made desolate.

The showers have come like a cool hand softly laid upon a fevered forehead. The rain has not been a very heavy one, and now there is a halt as though the elements were uncertain whether to continue their bounties. But the darkness cometh on apace; already with the shortening day I have to draw my chair close to the window to obtain light enough for my writing; I have faith to believe that the fountains will again be opened during the night watches.

I look out upon the leaves of the maple tree near my window, washed clean of the fine dust which has been borne upon the wings of the wind for many a day, and wonder what they are thinking all day long, and week after week, now hanging motionless and now swaying to and fro in the passing breeze. For that they have life is certain, and what is life without thought? I cannot quite rid myself of the feeling that there is a certain consciousness even in the leaves. Darwin has shown such acts of

deliberation upon the part of climbing
plants, as give us pause, and make us
occasionally feel that we must speak softly,
and perhaps be a little careful even of our
reflections in their presence. And have you
not heard how sometimes a great tree,
being athirst, will send its roots far around
a rock or a building to a well or spring, in
order to fetch it water ?

So when I go up into a high mountain,
where great oaks and lordly pines and hem-
locks wave, or find my way down through
a secluded valley where a clear brook
tumbles over smooth worn stones, under
overhanging grasses and fronds of fern,
where the forget-me-not lifts its blue eyes,
and the proud cardinal flower sparkles, I
cannot quite think that my coming brought
thither the first throb of conscious life.
And when I see the lily sending its delicate
searching filaments deep down among the
noisome masses of decay and seemingly
useless waste, and drawing thence the elements from which it elaborates a glory of
green leaf and spotless and fragrant blossom,
and then look upon "a lord of creation"
who should be " how noble in reason ! how
infinite in faculty ! in form and movement
how express and admirable ! in action how

like an angel! in apprehension how like
a god!" and see him confined to a petty
round, or filled with ignoble ambitions;
defacing the lovely front of nature, or
cramping the souls about him, and soiling
all the fair pages that he touches, with no
responsive thrill to all the life impulses with
which the universe is ever palpitating, I
hardly have room to wonder which has the
nobler thoughts, or which is the purer and
truer channel for the current of the infinite
life.

SEPTEMBER 8, 1894.

LII.

A DARK and sombre room, only lighted by a lamp which stands upon a table at one side covered with books, crucibles, alembics, retorts, and vessels of various kinds. Books arranged in cases along the walls. Sitting by the table, bowed over the books, a little old man with long grey hair and beard. Music by the orchestra; it is Gounod's. Then the old man sings, and in the melody and harmony the story of Dr. Faustus is unfolded.

You can paint in high key or in low, in black and white or in colour; tell your story in prose or in poetry, in a monotone or in melodious phrases; given the medium and keynote, and all falls into its place. We do not, it is true, usually sing our soliloquies with gesticulations, but this does not make the opera untrue. We have been transported to the kingdom of the muses, where this is the universal custom, that is all. And so it does not disturb us in the least that as memory retraces the days that

266 FROM A NEW ENGLAND HILLSIDE.

are gone, and imagination calls up pictures of the joys of the past, a great longing takes possession of the soul of the scholar to walk again the pleasant paths of youth, and Mephistopheles emerges from the studious gloom, and in harmonious accents tenders his uncanny services.

How often, and in how many forms, the story comes to us! How to hold fast to life and its joys; how to turn the hour glass, and see again the sands running gently from the full to the empty bulb. In fact and in fiction: Ponce de Leon in search of the fountain of youth; the alchemists and the Rosicrucians; Paracelsus; Claude Frollo in Victor Hugo's "Hunchback of Notre Dame"; the Illuminati in George Sand's "Consuelo" and "Countess de Rudolstadt" and out of them: the famous French physician of our own day, Brown-Sequard, with his elixir of life. Life! Life! More life and fuller is our cry, and we cling to the receding years as one clings to a rope while feeling himself drifting ever farther and farther from shore upon an ebbing tide.

But exert ourselves as we may, we are only conscious that like one caught by a devil-fish, whose every writhing tends but to tighten upon him the monster's tentacles, or like one sinking in a quicksand, whose struggles carry him deeper and deeper, our efforts to escape are worse than vain. Ever present with us is the vision of those who long ago slipped beyond the curtain which shrouds the vast unknown. We see them as they were; they said to us but „Auf Wiedersehen,“ and now, the river that parts us, once but a tiny thread, has grown so wide, so wide! How easy for some, is the way which for others is marked "No thoroughfare!" With an assured confidence, born, shall we say? of lack of reflection, they drop the pulseless hand, believing that next week, next year, a generation hence, they will grasp it again and take up life in unchanged relations. Happy dreamers! Did it ever occur to you to try to realize how the young mother who leaves her child a prattling babe, and meets him again in some other sphere, a hoary-headed nonagenarian, with his sons and his daughters, his grandchildren and great-grandchildren about him, shall orient herself, and take up the old relation? Ah! my friends, I fear that in that other land, that "undiscovered country from whose bourne no traveller returns," either idealism reigns, and each will dwell in a fully equipped world of his own, or we shall have to begin again where fate may leave us. As the tree falls, so shall it lie ; there is no retracing the steps which have been taken.

How to grow old gracefully is the problem. The slings and arrows of outrageous fortune may have whizzed for many a year around our devoted heads, and the scars which we could show, may be as numerous as the sands of the sea. But the desires and hopes of our youth still linger with us, as we linger, mayhap, superfluous upon the stage. Have you ever reversed your opera-glass in the midst of the play and watched the tiny actors afar off go through their mimic parts, and seemed to hear their voices likewise fade into the remote distance ? So we must sometimes realize with a shock that while through our glass of custom, which is ever ready, we see the youths about us so near that we can put our hand upon them, they in their turn, with the inexperience of youth, hold their glasses reversed, and view us far, far away, a mere reminiscence of a life which has been, our feeble voices just whispering on the breeze, a part of the accumulated burden of the past. We suddenly catch sight of our reflection in the mirror, and wonder what strange spell can have transformed us so. Do you remember the quandary of the little old woman?

> "But if it be I, as I do hope it be,
> I've a little dog at home, and he'll know me;
> If it be I, he'll wag his little tail,
> And if it be not I, he'll loudly bark and
>   wail!"

> Home went the little woman all in the dark,
> Up got the little dog, and he began to bark,
> He began to bark, so she began to cry,
> "Lauk-a-mercy on me, this is none of I!"

But, alas! I am afraid it must be I, all the same, or what is left of the I that was, out from which may have gone so much virtue, or so much weakness. Is the individual but a passive instrument, a medium only, through which power passes to effect its end, as the wire bears the electric current? Does he not sometimes transmute the force, so that motion, as it were, becomes heat, or electric power or attraction? Is he not a solvent, and may not his presence now and then cause a rearrangement of the atoms, and precipitate the fine gold?

Helmholtz is dead, — he whose strong hand reconstructed, or constructed *ab initio*, the theory of the persistence of force. Think of it; since he published his paper upon the "Conservation of force" in 1847,

the world, to philosophic eyes, has been
a new world, — and Helmholtz is dead.
Dead ! What is that ?

One generation passeth away, and another
cometh : —

> It is time to be old,
> To take in sail:

— Ah ! but is it just that ? Let us see that
our garments have a fitting modesty of
colour and form ; let us withdraw to a quiet
corner and release the younger spirits which
cannot brook long confinement.

> On with the dance ! let joy be unconfined ;
> No sleep till morn, when Youth and Pleasure
>   meet
> To chase the glowing hours with flying feet.

But when the passing years have been
accepted, and the sceptre has been surren-
dered into other hands, though we be old,
the world is yet young, and it has no retired list.

> As the bird trims her to the gale,
> I trim myself to the storm of time,
> I man the rudder, reef the sail,
> Obey the voice at eve obeyed at prime.

It is not well to be always analyzing one's
sensations and one's character ; seeds will

not germinate if they are dug up very often
to see whether they have yet sprouted.
But a good merchant occasionally takes
account of stock, and at all events he knows
that he must have a clear idea of the relation in which he stands to the market, and
to his associates and competitors. The
mariner takes an observation when the sun
crosses the line. It is worth while for a
man to know whether or not he is out of
his course; worth while to know whether
the light at his prow is playing the part of
a will-of-the-wisp and leading other craft
into dangerous waters. And, dropping the
simile, it is worth while to avoid being a
bore, a grumbler, a marplot, a busybody,
a burden or a nuisance of any kind; worth
while to remember that there is much to be
done by all who can work, before the human
race shall be all that the human race might
be, before the inhabited world shall be all
compact of grace and loveliness. So though

   — you and I are old;
Old age hath yet his honour and his toil;
Death closes all: but something ere the end,
Some work of noble note, may yet be done,
Not unbecoming men that strove with Gods.
The lights begin to twinkle from the rocks:
The long day wanes: the slow moon climbs:
   the deep

Moans round with many voices. Come,
    my friends,
'Tis not too late to seek a newer world.
Push off, and sitting well in order smite
The sounding furrows; for my purpose holds
To sail beyond the sunset, and the baths
Of all the western stars, until I die.
It may be that the gulfs will wash us down:
It may be we shall touch the Happy Isles,
And see the great Achilles, whom we knew.
Tho' much is taken, much abides; and tho'
We are not now that strength which in old
    days
Moved earth and heaven; that which we are,
    we are;
One equal temper of heroic hearts,
Made weak by time and fate, but strong in
    will
To strive, to seek, to find, and not to yield.

SEPTEMBER 15, 1894.

LIII.

I HAVE planted a bit of sky in the marshy ground at the foot of the pasture. When I put it there I could only see in it gray smoke and haze, with now and then a glint of blue, with coarse grass and golden-rods and asters reversed around the borders. But last night I found the whole moon in it. full and round, with two dainty stars, far, far down in the depths of the earth beneath, and to-day there are towering masses of cumulus cloud with frills and ripples along the edges, luminous above, and deepening below to a tone the real lightness of which you will never know until you undertake to paint it. You do not realize how delicate and graceful and subtile are the lines of tree and herb, until you watch their reflections in a sheet of water. Nature is so lavish of her beauty that it is usually with us all as it was with Yankee Doodle, who "Couldn't see the town for so many houses." We need to have a tiny morsel set apart and to concentrate our

T

attention upon it in order to see a little of
that grace of which the world is full.

I think if people only knew how much
easier it is to transplant the sky than it is
to transplant safely anything else, they
would always have a bit of it growing
within their line of vision. I mean people
who live in the country, that is, people who
actually live. Even those who *survive* in
the city, if they are so fortunate as to own
or rent a parallelepipedon (I believe that is
the word) twenty feet by a hundred, beginning at the centre of the earth and extend-
ing into infinite space, might plant a bit of
the sky in their back yard, and so get into
near relations with something that is pure
and true, if changeable. But I am wrong as
to the shape of these little tuppenny-ha'penny
city possessions. The sides are not parallel,
but instead, each starts from an invisible
point at the centre of the earth, and, reaching the designated size at the surface, continues to broaden and broaden out into
infinite space forever and ever, amen. And
the peculiarity of this little matter, infinity,
is that out there there is no need to quarrel
about boundaries, but how many soever
there may be of these closely packed municipal neighbours, though their number be

infinite, in the last extremity (which is never reached) each man's territory becomes infinite in length and breadth as well as in thickness. And so he has *his* escape into the infinite.

And it is worth something to see the sky, even at second hand. Worth, ah! how much! to look out upon great stretches of it, upon untold and untellable millions of miles, with its cloud-capped towers, its gorgeous palaces, its solemn temples.

We are now in the full tide of the early autumn, with its wealth of bloom. All the old favourites are here: the asters and the golden-rods, the cardinal flower, the fringed gentian, the ladies'-tresses, the grass of Parnassus, the wild carrot, the autumn buttercup, — a wealth of bloom that defies enumeration or computation or description. And the green trees also are putting on their ascension robes, not of white, but of brown and of red and of gold.

But the summer lingers; the air is still and sultry; portentous clouds gather on the hills beyond the valley, and are cloven from time to time by flashes of lightning, and heavy thunder rolls around the welkin.

SEPTEMBER 16, 1894.

LIV.

"THE rains descended and the floods came and the winds blew and beat upon that house, and it fell not." And it rained, and it rained, and it rained. It was really like old times. The rain came on rather gently and intermittently, but gradually gained force and continuity until after nightfall, and then we had it in earnest, a steady downpour. The fountains of the heavens were opened, and hour after hour the deluge fell, making glad the thirsting fields and the hearts of men. We remembered that in former times, under the old dispensation, we had had such rains, and there was a grateful sense of something familiar which had quite passed from our memory, but which had suddenly been again brought to mind.

The following morning the sun came out bright and clear. I went up the hill, passing upon my way the pool in the marsh, which I found full to the brim, and weeping over its low embankment. The cottage was in its place, but it held more water than I

hope it may ever hold again. The roof had
not been quite completed when the rain
began, and the temporary drains upon the
ungraded slope proved insufficient for the
emergency, so that a more than ample
supply was delivered through the cellar windows. But otherwise the building had not
suffered, and it was a small matter to open
the permanent drain already planned, and
draw off the accumulation, which for a
time formed a mountain torrent in the fore-
ground. The carpenters were stimulated to
renewed exertions by the warning, and set
to work in good earnest to close the gap in
the roof (the stable-door, as it were), a
labour which they had just completed upon
the coming of another heavy shower in the
afternoon.

The new grass has sprung up freely over
the field, and its fresh green gives a pleasant
overtone to the brown earth, which it does
not yet, but soon will, cover.

The day after the storm I placed in my
brooder twelve downy little youngsters that
had just been hatched, and sent the mother
off to attend to other business. It was my
first experiment with the brooder, though
I had kept it heated for several days to test
its temper. One of the infants had not

acquired quite strength enough to break
the shell, and was assisted in that under-
taking by Nicholas John. It was then put
into the brooder with the others. but seemed
so weak and miserable, thus thrown so
untimely upon a cold and uncharitable
world, that it was placed for a few hours
in the incubator. This, by the way, contains about a hundred eggs, the tenants of
which are at present something more than
half way between this world and the world
to come, or between the other world and
this, whichever is the more appropriate
expression. (I get very much confused between these different worlds.) The outcome
of this experiment will be very interesting.
However it may result with the eggs, the
effect was quite satisfactory in the case of
the immature chick, which, after being put
back into the brooder, I found busy with
the others, the following morning, all being
engaged in earning an honest livelihood on
the floor of their wooden foster mother.

Thinking them now old enough to endure
a further experience of life, I removed
the slide which closed the approach to the
sunny outer world; but it was an hour or
two before any ventured so far as into the
open air. At length I encouraged two or

three to go into the passageway, and then continued my work outside. After a while one gradually backed out of the passage, but it was some moments before it turned around and seemed to realize the new order of things. With head erect, it gazed upon the great universe, at the green leaves and the blue sky and the great sun, and I am sure it must have felt unutterable things. At all events, it did not utter any, and shortly afterward, with several others, it was busily engaged pecking away at the fresh earth near the mouth of the tunnel leading to its artificial foster mother. And before long, eleven little lumps of down, — brown and black and yellow, Brown Leghorn and Minorca and Light Brahma, were scattered around over quite a space of ground, as happily and naturally engaged as if they had not been introduced into this great world of ours a short ten minutes before.

I counted only eleven, and hearing a plaintive peep-peep-ing within, I examined and discovered that Benjamin, the poor foundling of the incubator, had not had courage to make a sortie, but, lost in the vast solitude of the otherwise empty box, was making his sad plight known in the manner most natural to him. Taking him up in my hand, I conveyed him into the yard, and put him down near the others, and after a few minutes of amaze and uncertainty he joined them in their busy investigation into the nature and character of the soil.

I was especially interested to note an exhibition of inherited, or so-called intuitive knowledge. One of the hens in the adjoining yard having given utterance to the familiar note of alarm and warning, the whole flock immediately huddled together at the mouth of the tunnel. And this reminds me of an incident that occurred a day or two since, which both interested and pleased me. A chicken several weeks old, and rather too large to get easily through the meshes of the wire netting, found itself within an inclosure where it was not intended to be, and tried in vain, with much vociferation, to get out. Seeing its difficulty, I went to its rescue, which I could only effect by catching it. This I did with some difficulty. While I was attempting to do this, its outcries were naturally redoubled, and that which especially pleased me was the fact that the whole flock of Plymouth Rocks on the other side of the net flew to its defence, and made a most vigorous, though vain, attack upon me for my supposed brutality. They only desisted when, having caught the chicken, I immediately released it among them, and I have no doubt that they then congratulated themselves upon having compelled me to suspend my nefarious proceedings.

SEPTEMBER 24, 1894.

LV.

Oh! Carry me back to ole Virginny.

This note is written really and truly from Underledge — far from Underledge. At the foot of the hill upon which stands the hotel, flow the turbid waters of the Roanoke, under broad-leaved buttonwoods and smaller-leaved persimmon trees. On the walls of the hotel the Allamanda vines make a great show, with their bright yellow blossoms, and on the terrace the crimson hibiscus and the motley lantana, with the broad-leaved banana and rich green rubber plant, make believe that they are in Bermuda. Around us the mountains rise in every direction, showing numerous conical peaks, the characteristic mountain forms of the picture books of our childhood. It is a new sensation to the eye accustomed to the long lines of the elevated table-lands of New England, to rest upon these forms, so different in their details, so distinctly mountainous. And as the mountains differ, so likewise

do all the other elements of the situation.
The southern colonel with his broad slouch
hat and his long legs and long beard, appears in great force. So does the southern
negro in all degrees of picturesqueness.
From an elevated office window I look
down upon the open market-place with its
ox-carts and its wagon loads of water-
" millions " and vegetables of all sorts ; and
in the court-house, where the general quietness and decorum in speech surprised me,
I have the opportunity to admire the skill
with which a learned advocate, in the
course of an impassioned address to the
jury, manages to " shoot off his mouth "
unerringly (I use the popular slang in a
literal sense) first in one direction and
then in another, at the spittoons stationed
many feet away from him, while I observe
evidences all around me of a lack of similar
skill upon the part of others.

As the train wound its circuitous way
through the Shenandoah valley two nights
ago, it seemed to pitch and roll almost like
a vessel in a storm at sea, insomuch as to
make walking from one end of the car to
another without support quite impossible ;
and even in one's berth, one was liable to
be overcome by qualms of conscience, — or

something else internal. But when morning dawned, the beauty of the scenery compelled attention to that alone. The foliage is yet but little changed by the coming of autumn, but the drought here has been very severe, and still continues. In the morning and the evening light, the mountain ranges take on an exquisite beauty of tone and colour. There is, however, in many places a sense of solitude and often of desolation, which is depressing. The latter as caused doubtless, in part at least, by the occurrences of the times when Sheridan was but "twenty miles away," is visible here and there in the ruins of what were probably at one time substantial and prosperous homesteads. At other points there are the even more discouraging monuments of the widespread real estate boom of a few years ago.

The characteristic building throughout most of the valley is the old log house, usually more or less dilapidated, but occasionally carefully plastered between the logs so as to produce the effect of a section of a zebra, set up on end. Often these appear as a collection or line of negro cabins placed near the bottom upon each side of a narrow valley or ravine, where the old mammies stand in the doorways, or the little pickaninnies lie around basking in the sun. There is seldom any evidence of effort to beautify the home-place by the planting of trees, shrubs, or vines, or otherwise. The surroundings are usually bare and unsightly. The house has the appearance not of a home as we think of it, but of being a mere shelter from the inclemency of the elements. This is doubtless largely because of the great poverty of the people, which everywhere forces itself upon the attention ; but it cannot be only because of this. Certainly in other localities you frequently find unmistakable evidences of poverty accompanied by like unmistakable evidences of a craving for something more than food, clothing, and the shelter of a roof.

"The man on horseback" is seen everywhere where people are visible. The saddle is a natural home for a Virginian. I cannot, however, say much for the grace and comeliness of the ordinary Virginia horse as I have seen him during the past few days. I am inclined to think that he must rather yield the palm to the mule, whose long ears make their appearance upon every side. Not many unfamiliar crops appear in the fields. The tobacco that I have seen would make a very poor showing alongside that of Connecticut or Massachusetts, but I cannot think that that which I have seen can fairly represent the region. Much of the corn crop has been cut and stacked in shocks. That which has not been cut has had the stalks above the ears removed, and the ears hanging down, the fields have taken on a dejected appearance. An occasional field of ripening millet is perhaps the most unfamiliar agricultural feature which has attracted my attention.

Here, in a great railroad centre, there is a sense of incongruity in the mixture of northern and southern elements, the *laissez faire* of the natives, and the "get there" of the invading Yankees. I cannot say that either of them in the present stage impresses me very pleasantly; but then I suppose that it is characteristic of the born optimist that to him the things of the present are always pretty bad — else how could he be ever looking forward to the times when things will be better? "There's a good time coming, boys; wait a little longer."

September 25, 1894.

LVI.

As I write, I am sitting under the magnificent arch of the Natural Bridge. I have made the ordinary round, following a lateral stream from the hotels, past the great old gnarled arbor vitæ trees, to Cedar creek, and thence up along its course through the gorge, under the great arch, to the saltpetre cave, to Hemlock Island, to Lost River, and Lace Water Falls. Then by devious ways among great tulip and hemlock and beech trees and along and over steep hillsides, I gained the ruined summer house or observatory from whence one can see in all directions a multitudinous host of mountains: Purgatory Mountain and House Mountain, North Mountain and Cave Mountain, and scores of others, with the famed Peaks of Otter away in the southeast. Numerous cones appear from this point, as from almost every other in the valley. The view is superb.

And then, still following the beaten track,

I came out at length upon the top of the bridge, whence its imposing height is more clearly discerned. The stream beneath has suffered greatly from the long drought. When it is full, as during the breaking up of the accumulated snows of the winter, the view must be most effective from this point.

Here I parted from a chance travelling acquaintance, and struck off into a bypath through the woods, trusting that it would ultimately lead me to an easy slope by which I might make my descent again to the bed of the stream, and in this I was not mistaken. And so, following now the conventional path, now stepping or springing from rock to rock in the bed of the creek, and now pushing my way among trees and bushes, I at last find myself alone in the fading evening light under the bridge itself, with no sound in my ears but that of the water as it makes its way over its irregular rocky bed.

It is good to be here, — good to look up at that vast arch with the pictures of which we have all been so familiar from childhood, but which so few of us see or think that we much care to see. Let me tell you to go to see it, and also to do what I cannot

do, remain long enough to know it in its
various aspects, and to steep yourself fully
in the beauty of this most beautiful region.

Having a reverent regard for the memory of the father of his. and my country,
I have been trying — in vain — to discover
the point where that distinguished citizen
carved his name upon the bridge, an act
in the performance of which I sincerely
wish that he had been the last. He seems
to have been as ready with his knife as
with his hatchet. And I have also been
thinking, reminded thereby of Robert
Lowell's poem, "Fresh Hearts that Failed
Three Thousand Years ago," with its
motto, "Men that were makers" its story
of the long and weary climb, and its pa-
thetic ending, — "A boy — and yet no
name." Here, indeed, carved upon the
rock was the name of a man who was a
maker, the maker of an empire; who left
behind him, to last as long as records may
endure and after this great bridge shall
have crumbled into the valley, a name to
be remembered.

But what boots it? What is fame that
we should greatly desire it? It is pleasant
to have the recognition of those whom you
know, of your countrymen, of your genera-

U

tion ; but better is it to know or to trust in the secrecy of your own heart, that you are at least one of the men who are makers, — that in an evil time, you have laid a stone or carried mortar or borne a message which contributed to the strengthening of the empire which your forefathers builded. Grateful is it to the spirit — at least grateful it should be — to do something toward the construction of an enduring bridge between the glories of the past and the greater glories of the future. Pontifex Maximus only one can be ; let us make sure that each of us can name himself in his most secret hour pontifex — and therewith be content.

SEPTEMBER 26, 1894.

LVII.

THE scene changes. I am again at Underledge. And after making allowance for all that is sordid and mean in our life, for the selfishness and self-seeking, for the ignoble ambitions, for the waste of thought and precious hours upon petty things, for the prevalent crude materialism which takes little note of the higher matters of the imagination, for the dull æsthetic sense which leads to the most frightful monstrosities in omission and commission, at which you will bear me witness that I have not hesitated to grumble, I am bound to admit that I approach my home with an assurance that there are degrees in degradation, and that we are not at the lowest depth. Industry is a good thing, and we are more industrious. Thrift is a good thing, and we are more thrifty. Extended knowledge is a good thing, and we know more of the world. Neatness is a good thing, and we are more neat. Beauty is a good thing, and we strive in a way for beauty, and sometimes achieve it, even if our ways are often mistaken ones.

And I think that this is true not only of an old village such as this, old in the American sense, I mean, but I think that it is also true of the more retired regions of the Eastern States, whence cities are not readily accessible, where the demands of life are hard, and where intercommunication between families and neighbourhoods is difficult.

I am fain to believe that another generation will effect considerable changes, and changes for the better, in the region that I have just left. Therefore I live in hope. I saw there two distinct phases of life, — the old life which suffers under the *vis inertiæ*, and which has hardly awakened to the present, and the disagreeable new life of what seems almost like a border town (although in fact one of the oldest in the country), because it has recently been invaded by the speculative immigrant from the North, with all his shrewdness, and all his lack of "sweetness and light." But grace and beauty are sure to blossom in the end.

At the extreme south end of our village, upon a low mound at the foot of a beautiful green slope, below one of the finest points of the ledge, which is here, as at most other points, masked by forest trees, there stands a large farmhouse built about a hundred years ago. It is painted white, with green blinds, in the ordinary New England fashion, and is surrounded by trees; and from the front, and the wide veranda at the side, there is an uninterrupted view across the valley to the western hills, which, as I looked upon them to-day just after the sun had sunk behind them, lay firmly outlined on the clear evening sky.

This is what we know as "The Lodge." It is one of the numerous holiday homes established in late years, for the benefit of those whose ordinary life is that of the shop and the tenement-house, many of whom, doubtless, had no clear idea of what the world was where there were no paved streets and blocks of houses, until the opportunity offered which these homes afford. This one is supported by the alumnæ and others interested in our seminary, who supply it with guests and watch over it with loving care. In it twenty young women and girls can be accommodated at once, and fresh relays are sent from time to time during the summer. They will be received, indeed, at any season, but with the coming on of the cooler weather comes the bustle and hurry of business, and few can then escape from their accustomed toils. Indeed, the country in winter is a *terra incognita* to most citizens, — even those whose occupations do not tie them to the cities, — if I were not constitutionally opposed to puns, I should say a terror incognita. If it were otherwise, and they really knew how beautiful the winter is, the exodus from the cities would be so great that we should have to go to them to find elbow room, excepting that the country — "all out of doors" — is so broad and hospitable. As it is, even in summer time and on the border of our village, some find it very lonesome at their first coming.

The lodge has now been used as such for about ten years. It is under the direct charge of a farmer well on in middle life (who was born in it), and his wife, who are thus enabled to remain in their old home, and at the same time effectively serve the purpose of those responsible for the venture.

It is pleasant to meet the pale inmates strolling in the sun, and feel that some of the humours of their common life are being exorcised, and a more healthy tone, moral and physical, is being established. And whatever the dangers of ordinary charity in the way of almsgiving or otherwise, I think that none can find solid ground for effective criticism of an enterprise like this.

SEPTEMBER 29, 1894.

LVIII.

SIXTY-NINE dear little fuzzy foundlings have graduated from the incubator. There should have been more, but, as fate would have it, some never got "out of the everywhere into the here," and some, like numerous other promising enterprises of great pith and moment, "died-a-bornin'."

And after all, the result of this first experiment is far from being contemptible. As the time approached for it to culminate, my watchfulness increased, and I hovered over the machine and its precious contents with a truly motherly interest and anxiety. On the evening of the twentieth day, by intently listening, I could just hear the slightest tap-tapping of the prisoners upon the walls of their cells, and it was not until the next morning that the three boldest made their appearance, having accomplished the Monte Cristo trick and emancipated themselves for good or for ill. And awkward little miserable sinners they were.

Throughout that day and the next the

flock continued to grow, lots being transferred to the brooder from time to time as
soon as they appeared to have got their sea
legs on, until all had been consigned to its
shelter. And a quizzical looking company
they were, but withal disposed rapidly to
put on the air of knowing it all, as if a
mother were of no account, and collectivism
were the only wear. And lively little ap-
petites they have, and they know exactly
what to do with their bills. Should the
weather prove fair to-morrow, the trap door
will be opened, and then ho! for the world,
the beautiful world!

My dainty Aramis, my Amadis de Gaul,
Thaddeus of Warsaw, Baron Trenck, Cas-
anova, or whatever name he may be most
pleased to be called, has fallen from his
high estate. It is slanderously said that
every man has his price, and if this be
so, with some doubtless the price depends
upon the æsthetic sense.

The Leghorns are moulting, the last of
the tribes. And a sorry lot they are, all
save one. Even the prince himself shows
a shabby tail, bereft of its graceful sickles;
but die Frauen are, as the phrase goes, a
sight to behold. During their days of prosperity my gentleman maintained his courtly

demeanour, but the present situation imposes too great a strain upon his nerves. The only lady who still continues to dress well, or who has passed through the day of small things, I am not sure which, is permitted to eat from the same dish with him, and comes forward without hesitation. But woe unto the miserable dowdies that venture to pick up a crumb under my lord's eye. They are put to the right about, and sent packing without ceremony.

Alas! that it should be so. Certainly in so well regulated a family the motto should be, bear and forbear, — but I must record the situation as it is. And let us have charity, and remember that we are necessarily subject to the defects of our virtues. Here is one of those high-strung cases where culture carries its own penalty. There are many such. I have known musical people suffer much from performances from which I was ignorant enough to thrill with pleasure.

OCTOBER 4, 1894.

LIX.

One-ery, two-ery, hickory Ann,
Phillis and Phollis and Nicholas John,
Que-by, Qua-by, Sister Mary,
Single 'em, Sangle 'em, Buck begone!

It was just a year ago yesterday that I
wrote the first of these encyclical letters.
As then, this morning was bright and
sunny, but it was cold, and with frost in
the lowlands. The day has continued absolutely cloudless, save just enough at sunset to let it end in glory, — the sky a dome
of perfect blue.

Looking from the terrace, I see that
October has been tinting the foliage here
and there, now a touch of yellow or orange
en a sassafras, and now scarlet and gold on
a maple, or crimson upon sumach or wood-
bine. In the steely atmosphere the lines
of the hills come out sharp and clear, and
even those upon my farthest horizon, thirty
miles away, approach to a friendly nearness.

I have tried many of the roads and paths
which cross the valleys and climb the hills,

ever finding new beauties to rejoice in and more simple marvels to wonder at. I trust that I shall continue to wander into new paths this many a day, and I am sure that I shall not exhaust them, for their name is legion. But over yonder is a mountain of which I shall never see the other side. It is my Carcassone. I am sure that this mountain conceals wonderful things. I think that there I should find the happy valley for which weary men so long have sought. But I shall not explore the recesses of this valley. I shall continue, I hope, year after year to look up to the summit of the mountain and picture the wonders that the valley contains, and the joys of those that dwell therein, and I shall marvel at those wonders, and luxuriate in those joys so long as I live. The valley shall be to me the valley of dreams.

October is painting the drop curtain, and upon the Æolian harp at the window the freshening breeze is singing the swan song of the waning year. And thinking of the days that are lately gone, of the new friendships that have come into being, never, I am sure, to be ended, and of the purer and truer thoughts that have come out of the inmost life of Nature; touching with a caressing hand the old gray rocks that have so kindly lent themselves to build the cottage walls, and gazing out upon the beautiful world, which is already so old, and yet so new that I look upon it each day with a fresh surprise, it seems to me that I may fairly say, "The lines are fallen unto me in pleasant places; yea I have a goodly heritage."

A year has slipped away into the silences, — gone to lie in that great mausoleum where the vanished years shall rest for aye.

"Sergeant, call the roll."

All present, or accounted for. Our highways and our byways are bright again with Tam o' Shanter and scarf and ribbon; the light-hearted equestriennes chase each other over the hills; merry voices break musically upon the evening air; the blinds are thrown back, the cobwebs brushed away, the pleasant halls of learning are reopened. From Holland and the Swiss lakes and mountains, and from the green lanes of Merrie England come these, those from neighbouring city or town, or from the boundless West, where Nature seems to do everything with a lavish hand, and upon a mighty scale in keeping with the magnitude of that great empire.

All present, or accounted for. But some are scattered to the four winds about their various missions, and some tarry under the shadow of the eternal snows which lie upon the massive flanks and upon the Aiguilles of the Alps. And here and there, there are fresh graves, and there are some which though distant are often present to our memory which are not fresh, but upon which the grass grows thick and long, and over which the eglantine strews its petals. We look wistfully into the vast unknown, if haply we may catch a glimpse of the presence which we miss, and there remains a touch of the old heartache, but we close up the ranks, and feel more tenderly the ties that bind us to those that are left.

> As through the land at eve we went,
>   And pluck'd the ripen'd ears,
> We fell out, my wife and I,
> O, we fell out, I know not why,
>   And kiss'd again with tears.
> For when we came where lies the child
>   We lost in other years,
> There above the little grave,
> O, there above the little grave,
>   We kiss'd again with tears.

My friend once told me: "Old fellow, you should not wear your heart upon your sleeve. Any one could see from your last note that you had been going through deep waters."

Ah, but suppose you must?

Longfellow says, —

Look then into thine heart, and write!

and Lowell: —

" I consider every poem I write (whether I publish it or not) as a letter to all those whom I personally hold dear. I feel that I have made a truer communication of myself so than in any other way — that is, that I have in this way written my friends a letter from the truer and better J. R. L., who resides within, and often at a great distance from, the external man, who has some good qualities, but whose procrastination is enough to swamp them all."

Shall we write the things that we feel, or the things that we do not feel? I pray you, let us not fear to be honest. Do not be a cry-baby if you can help it, but if you love your friend, tell him so; if he is in trouble, put your arm about him; and if you get nipped between the upper and the nether millstones, do not hesitate to let him know the fact.